D0349745

THE 7 Minute MARRIAGE SOLUTION

THE 7 Minute MARRIAGE SOLUTION

**7 Things to Stop! 7 Things to Start!
7 Minutes That Matter Most!**

STEPHEN ARTERBURN

Best-selling author of *Every Man's Battle*

WORTHY
PUBLISHING

Copyright © 2013 by Stephen Arterburn

Published by Worthy Publishing, a division of Worthy Media, Inc., 134 Franklin Road, Suite 200, Brentwood, Tennessee 37027.

HELPING PEOPLE EXPERIENCE THE HEART OF GOD

Library of Congress Control Number: 2012941810

eBook available at worthypublishing.com

Audio distributed through Brilliance Audio; visit brillianceaudio.com

All rights reserved. No portion of this book may be reproduced, stored in a retrieval system, or transmitted in any form or by any means—electronic, mechanical, photocopy, recording, scanning, or other—except for brief quotations in critical reviews or articles, without the prior written permission of the publisher.

Unless otherwise noted, Scripture quotations are taken from *The Holy Bible*, New Living Translation. © 1996. Used by permission of Tyndale House Publishers, Inc., Wheaton, Illinois 60189. All rights reserved.

Scripture quotations marked NIV are taken from the Holy Bible, New International Version®. Copyright © 1973, 1978, 1984, 2010 by Biblica, Inc.™ Used by permission of Zondervan. All rights reserved worldwide. www.zondervan.com

Scripture quotations marked NKJV are taken from the New King James Version. © 1982 by Thomas Nelson, Inc. Used by permission. All rights reserved.

Scripture quotations taken from the King James Version are public domain.

For foreign and subsidiary rights, contact Riggins International Rights Services, Inc.; rigginsrights.com

ISBN: 978-1-93603-462-8 (hardcover w/ jacket)
ISBN: 978-1-61795-234-0 (international edition)

Cover Design: Christopher Tobias, Tobias' Outerwear for Books
Interior Typesetting: Susan Browne Design

Printed in the United States of America

13 14 15 16 17 CGFF 8 7 6 5 4 3 2 1

To my wife:
You are giving me the best years of my life.
As my mother said before we married,
"Everyone should be married to someone like you."
Well, I am, and I'm so grateful.

CONTENTS

Fixing Your Marriage Is Easier Than You Think 1

FIXING YOUR MARRIAGE IS EASIER THAN YOU THINK

To watch a short video on this subject, go to
7MinuteMarriageSolution.com/intro

When you saw the title *The 7 Minute Marriage Solution*, your first impulse may have been, "You've got to be kidding—a seven-minute solution to my marriage? No way!" It sounds too good to be true.

But having a strong marriage isn't as complicated as you think. Yes, we all have issues with our mates, but overall, we make marriage ridiculously harder than it has to be.

If we're honest with ourselves, we all know the self-defeating thoughtless things we do every day.

- We use put-down humor or criticize our mate in public.
- We try to change our mate into the "perfect" spouse.
- We run up credit-card debt or secretly spend money.
- We nag and complain about our mate's flaws.
- We manipulate, give the silent treatment, or say harsh things in anger.
- We hold grudges and refuse to forgive our mate's mistakes.

A strong marriage is one in which both partners *stop* doing negative behaviors and start doing positive ones.

In order to identify the most harmful and most helpful behaviors in marriage, we conducted a national survey of randomly selected adults who were either married or formerly married (some Christians and some not), inquiring about things spouses ought to stop doing or start doing to make a marriage work. Interestingly, the survey revealed that no matter the age, marital status, or spiritual background of the respondents, they listed the same seven most important things to start and seven things to stop doing to improve their marriage. Even more interestingly, all the respondents—both women and men—agreed on the number-one most important thing to start doing in marriage.

In this book, I've combined the eye-opening results of this national survey with several years of extensive study based on hundreds of couples' experiences in our New Life Marriage Weekend workshops, a research project from the Center for Bible Engagement, and my own personal experience. The result is a plan that shows you how to uproot the seven most harmful behaviors in your marriage and how to implement the seven most helpful behaviors. When you and your spouse also incorporate the seven most important minutes of the day, your marriage will be transformed.

Having a strong marriage comes down to this:

7 things to stop.
7 things to start.
7 minutes that matter most.

This 7 + 7 + 7 plan goes beyond what makes a marriage better and moves it to become a whole new relationship.

You might think a seven-minute marriage solution sounds overly simplistic: "Sure, this plan looks good on paper, but it will never work in real life."

I assure you, this is far more than a clever formula or mere theory. I've actually watched this 7 + 7 + 7 plan produce dramatic results in real marriages. In our New Life Marriage Weekend workshops, couples who had signed divorce papers tore them up. After being separated for years, husbands and wives moved back in together. Angry and alienated spouses fell in love again.

Plus, these principles have strengthened my own marriage. This 7 + 7 + 7 plan brought us through some tough times and left us with a very connected, deeply intimate, and extremely satisfying relationship. I was telling my wife, Misty, the other night that I have never loved or felt love like this. At one time I had given up on the hope of a marriage like this. I want you to experience this kind of relationship also. You don't have to be walking out the door and toward divorce to use this plan. *The 7 Minute Marriage Solution* will take a pretty good marriage to an even greater level of satisfaction.

No matter what your relationship is like right now, this 7 + 7 + 7 plan will transform your marriage.

If you put into practice the simple strategies contained in these chapters, you will be amazed at what will happen. You and your spouse will connect with God and each other in a way that few couples have experienced. You will be united in a powerful three-way bond that will not be easily broken.

Whether you have a struggling marriage or a good marriage that you want to be even better, everything you need is contained right here. If you and your spouse are willing to take a look at these core issues and do some things differently, you can have the strong marriage you've always wanted.

PART ONE

THINGS TO STOP

1

[STOP CLINGING]
TO UNREALISTIC
EXPECTATIONS

To watch a short video on this subject, go to
7MinuteMarriageSolution.com/1

In the 2001 chick flick *The Wedding Planner*, Matthew McConaughey plays Dr. Steve Edison, a pediatrician, and Jennifer Lopez is Mary Flore, a wedding planner hired by a female client engaged to Steve. Steve is not with his fiancée during the initial stages of planning the wedding, so he and Mary do not meet. Later they encounter each other accidentally, but Mary does not know he is the groom of her client. The attraction between them is immediate, and they spend a romantically charged evening enjoying a community event in the local park.

Mary instantly falls in love with Steve—or at least in love with the idea of being in love with him. But when she discovers that he is the groom of her client, she is angry and hurt because she believes he has deceived her. A love-hate relationship ensues. But Steve, now attracted to Mary, comes to believe he is not as in love with his bride-to-be as he thought. The movie ends with this realization blossoming moments before the ceremony as Steve breaks off the wedding, rushes to find Mary, and they get married—supposedly to live happily ever after.

It's a fun, romantic movie that's typical of most in its genre. But I believe movies of this type—along with the TV shows, magazines, and romance novels of the past half-century—have done much to create the seriously flawed expectations couples take into marriage today. I am convinced that these unrealistic expectations are a major cause of the ballooning number of failed marriages in America.

Studies show that most Americans (70 percent) believe the purpose of marriage is to find a mate who will make them happy.[1] By "happy" they mean that marriage should sustain consistently romantic feelings between soul mates whose sexual ecstasy lasts a lifetime. Of course, this is not the reality of day-to-day married life. Yet many newlyweds cling to these unrealistic expectations. Therefore, the first argument creates a crisis rather than being just a normal event through which great marriages grow.

Unrealistic expectations are toxic in marriage. Stable marriages require both partners to take a hard look at mutual goals, compatibility on practical matters, and deep commitment to shared values, religion, and moral principles.

I find it significant that in *The Wedding Planner*, Steve and Mary do not take the time to get to know each other intimately. Their backgrounds, parentage, values, religion, goals, undiscovered personality traits, or economic expectations are not considered. They don't know if they both want children or if they act like children when they don't get their way. The message of the movie is that love conquers all, and nothing else matters as long as the couple's kisses curl their toes (or in most current movies, their lovemaking sets off fireworks). Steve and Mary believe they are each other's romantic soul mate, so all other concerns will automatically fall into place.

If it turns out that the marriage does not make them happy, they conclude they must have chosen the wrong mate. So they divorce and begin a new search for their romantic soul mate. (Or perhaps more commonly, first find their new romantic soul mate and then get a divorce.)

Unrealistic Expectations Undermine Reality

I believe in love and romance as much as anyone. But the unrealistic expectations created by making romance the primary focus of your relationship can lead to an early unraveling of the marriage bond.

Over and over I have seen people enter marriage expecting nonstop romantic bliss, and within a few weeks they are surprised by how difficult it is to live together harmoniously. Often the couple clings to these fantasy expectations because they didn't date long enough to know each other well. When expectations are dashed by harsh reality, the marriage spirals into a miserable existence of disappointment, regret, and resentment.

YOU AND YOUR SPOUSE CAN LIVE HAPPILY EVER AFTER—BUT ONLY IF BOTH OF YOU ARE WILLING TO WORK THROUGH THE ISSUES AND DIFFERENCES YOU BROUGHT INTO THE MARRIAGE.

You and your spouse *can* live happily ever after—but only if both of you are willing to work through the issues and differences you brought into the marriage. You hear little or nothing about this struggle in the movies or pop literature. What if Mary intends to keep her wedding-planning career while Steve expects her to be a stay-at-home mom? What if she never reckoned on his long hours and 3 a.m. emergencies that are standard in the life of a doctor? What if another beautiful woman turns Steve's head as easily as Mary turned his?

Again, these dashed expectations result from too little time spent getting to know the other person. Before marriage, both put their best foot forward, and the other foot is not exposed until after the honeymoon. And each partner is shocked to see how ugly that other foot turns out to be.

When Robert and Frances were dating, he was always kind and gentle with her. Once she had found a stack of old newspapers on Robert's car seat and, assuming they were trash, pitched them into a sidewalk receptacle. She didn't realize that the papers were his collection of clippings about his college tennis career. When he discovered the loss, he had been upset but understanding. He made no complaint about the humiliation of having to rummage through the trash can to retrieve his treasures.

But one Saturday morning less than a month after they married, Robert was out golfing and Frances decided to do him the favor of organizing his cluttered desk. She was careful to throw away nothing. When Robert came home he went ballistic, cursing and belittling her for messing with his stuff and invading his privacy. It was only the first of many such explosions, revealing a short-fused temper she had never suspected.

Had the haze of romantic expectations not dimmed her insight, Frances might have recognized hints of Robert's temper before they married, in the way he treated his mother or restaurant waiters, or even in the way he railed at drivers who tailgated, drove too slowly, or failed to signal turns. (Driving behavior provides an amazing number of clues to a person's inner character.) But with her he had kept his temper hidden until the daily reality of marriage revealed it.

Problems that surface during courtship don't go away; they intensify after you say "I do." In today's self-focused culture, marriage rarely serves as a channel for couples to grow and mature. Instead couples view marriage as their rightful opportunity to reap the rewards from their investment in courtship. The excitement of romantic pursuit and discovery gives way to a relaxing of the intense focus on pleasing each other. That's when harsh realities rise to the surface.

The Disappointment of the Soul-Mate Model

Disappointment with your mate is usually not caused by a dramatic character flaw or extreme self-centeredness, but merely by personal differences. Minor differences that seemed unimportant while dating expand into mountains of disappointment in marriage. Perhaps in the evenings you like to spend hours surfing the Internet, while your spouse wants to watch movies together. Your mate likes to watch sitcoms; you want to flip to the news. You believe you should eat only health foods; your spouse wants burgers and fries. Your mate loves NASCAR; you love symphonies.

While dating, you and your mate couldn't be together enough. But now that you are married and together all the time, you miss your independence and want more time to yourself. So you work late in the evenings and devote more time to your hobbies, causing your spouse to feel lonely. Or maybe your spouse feels smothered by your persistent desire for sex and becomes unresponsive to your sexual hints and advances. Maybe you revert to previous sloppy habits while your mate is an obsessive neatnik. You two don't go out as much in the evenings and eat fewer dinners together. One or both of you is grumpy in the morning or uncommunicative after a hard day's work.

If you and your spouse were seduced by the soul-mate model of marriage, you have no warning that the iceberg of unrealistic expectations looms ahead; thus, when you encounter it your hope sinks. How can you keep your marriage afloat? Couples whose relationships were formed on the soul-mate model feel blindsided by this harsh reality in marriage, and the resulting disappointment often brings dissatisfaction with the relationship and the beginning of a wandering eye.

If your marriage relationship is cooling because of unmet expectations, ask yourself this: Just what were you in love with—a fantasy of your own creation or a real person possessing the same fallen tendencies as every son of Adam and daughter of Eve? Did you fall in love with a person or with a feeling? As a golden oldie song put it, were you merely "falling in love with love"?

Resetting Your Expectations

Since the romantic soul-mate model for marriage creates false expectations that lead to disappointment, what are the right expectations that bind couples together in an enduring, satisfying, and happy marriage?

The traditional view of marriage held by most Americans until the end of of the twentieth century was this: "raising a family together, offering mutual aid to one another in tough times, and becoming engaged in larger networks of kin and community."[2] If you are clinging to the soul-mate model, the traditional model of marriage may seem overly practical and unromantic. But the bottom line is that it worked. Those marriages— built on a foundation of family, mutual aid, and community—tended to last a lifetime. The traditional model may seem to be a letdown from the romantic ecstasy promised by the soul-mate model. But that is only because both models have been misunderstood.

In suggesting you embrace the traditional model of marriage, I am not asking you to lower your expectations; I'm actually asking you to raise them. Marriage can be so much better than the soul-mate model has led you to expect. Marriage is not one-dimensional, focused solely on romance and sexual ecstasy. In reality, marriage is multidimensional, consisting of a series of seasons from the honeymoon to the empty nest during which the couple progresses from biological fireworks to deep, sustaining, romantic love and fruitful lives of shared experiences and relationships.

A marriage built on the traditional model embraces the big picture of all that marriage can be. If you want a strong marriage, stop clinging to unrealistic expectations of perpetual candlelight dinners and unending fireworks in the bedroom. Replace that expectation with the higher model of making your marriage the crowning achievement of a lifetime.

Differences in Gender

Another source of unrealistic expectations in a marriage is expecting your spouse to behave and respond to circumstances the same way you do—or the way your same-sex friends do. This expectation ignores the obvious reality of gender differences between men and women. Not only do you and your mate have different bodies, but you have differently wired brains, different emotional responses, and different hormones flooding your systems. This is why author John Gray says it's like men and women are from two different planets. When husbands and wives relate to each other, all these differences come into play and act as filters through which we perceive the other person. Naturally, each sex thinks its perspective is the accurate one. Yet men and women are inherently different, and if a spouse does not accept the differences, disappointment is a sure thing.

Let's take one common complaint as an example. Many women tell me about their husband's reticence to share his desires, fears, and problems. Viewing their husbands through a feminine filter, they interpret this reluctance as resistance to the intimacy she desires. "He's closed himself off to me," she complains, feeling rejected and hurt. While lack of communication is a flaw that many men need to work on, expecting a husband to share as deeply and fully as a female best friend is an unrealistic expectation that often leads to frustration and disappointment.

It's not that men don't have these feelings; most men love their wives dearly. But many men are like the old Vermont farmer who said, "I love my wife, Millie, so much it's all I can do to keep from telling her." The right feelings are there, and it would do wonders for a wife if he would let them out.

I am not excusing this reticence because I've learned that most women love expressions of endearment like flowers need rain. Of course, each woman is unique in how she prefers her husband to express his endearment. Perhaps she feels loved when you buy her a gift. Or she may feel loved when you write her a special note. Maybe she just wants you to spend time with her. The point for husbands is this: learn how your wife wants to be loved, and express your love to her that way.

We men do have our gender tendencies, but we don't have to be slaves to them. Each sex can learn a few new tricks for the sake of the other. But the point is, neither you nor your mate will get everything you dream of in the other. Both of you must be ready to accept traits that you wish were otherwise.

The best way to accept some gender differences is to learn to look at them as blessings. The truth is, neither sex will ever completely understand the other. It's simply not meant to be. Those differences are by God's design. Just as you and your mate can have a sexual relationship only because of your physical differences, many of the other ways you relate to each other are possible or at least enhanced because of differences—differences in outlook, ideas, abilities, and interests. If you and your spouse were exactly alike, you wouldn't need each other any more than you need two heads. Your world would be a dull place of limited horizons because you would be deprived of all the creativity, personalities, and development that come from the two of you pooling your differing outlooks, ideas, and abilities.

A key to a successful marriage is to learn not only to accept each other's gender differences, but also to use them to broaden the possibilities of what your marriage can become.

Differences in Family Background

We relate to each other not only through the filters of our respective genders but also of our family backgrounds and training. The two of you were raised in different homes, with different parents, siblings, friends, educations, and usually different churches—sometimes different denominations or even different religions. These varying influences leave each of you with different expectations.

In his family, for example, the kitchen was the woman's realm, and men were not expected to be part of it. In her family, the father helped in the kitchen. He took out the trash, mopped the floors, helped with the dishes, and often cooked steaks on the grill. Thus when the daughter from this family marries the son from the other, these differing expectations will be deeply embedded, likely causing friction over kitchen duties if they don't address the issue and develop kitchen duties that work for both of them.

One important reality every couple must learn to accept is each other's family. This is not always easy, and it often requires a generous dose of grace. Your mate's family may or may not have serious flaws, but they will certainly have significant differences that can cause misunderstandings. Often difficulties with a spouse's family are visible before the marriage, but the couple dismisses them as unimportant, saying, "I'm not marrying her parents; I'm marrying her." That is a myth. Relationships with parents are inevitable and can present problems neither partner expected.

Perhaps she's an only child from an academic family with quiet habits and reserved interactions. He's one of five siblings who love loud banter, jokes, competitive games, and raucous laughter. Expect misunderstandings in the marriage. Maybe his less-than-mature mother resented the transfer of his affections to his bride. Or her father disapproved of the marriage, thinking no man is good enough for his daughter—especially you. Expect problems. Scheduling family events can become as treacherous as walking through a minefield. His family thinks they should come home every Christmas. So does hers. Solutions are almost impossible, and relationships can get sticky. When you marry, you take your mate's family as your own and work toward loving and accepting them just as your mate does—warts, skeletons, inconveniences, and all.

DON'T HANG ON TO AN UNREALISTIC
EXPECTATION THAT THE OTHER PERSON IS
THERE TO MEET EVERY NEED YOU HAVE.

When dealing with the natural differences that arise from gender and backgrounds, it helps to be objective and realize that many perceived flaws in your mate are likely nothing more than unmet expectations on your own part. He may never earn the money to live in the style you hoped for, or she may not have the cooking skills or sexual interest you dreamed of. Don't hang on to an unrealistic expectation that the other person is there to meet every need you have. Accept and celebrate the differences.

The Reward of Realistic Expectations

Does focus on achieving the higher and more satisfying expectations of a full, blessed, lifelong relationship mean that you should dismiss romance as unimportant? Absolutely not! Take this higher, harder road to marital bliss and you are in for a happy surprise. It's hard for young people to imagine, but a silver-haired grandmother is likely to have a far stronger love for her balding, overweight husband stretched out in his recliner than she could possibly have imagined in their courting days. Those feelings are the result of a life built together through thick and thin, ups and downs, joy and tears. It's a much higher, broader, deeper, and more satisfying and tightly bound love than one based solely on romantic sensations and orgasmic intensity.

A strong marriage takes work, but the rewards are profound and abundant. Expect constant romance and you kill it, just as too much sugar makes you sick. But when you stop focusing only on romantic feelings and start being willing to iron out the wrinkles and smooth out the bumps, you'll find that you get lasting romance thrown in as a bonus.

Remember this truth from Proverbs 10:28: "The hopes of the godly result in happiness, but the expectations of the wicked come to nothing." Be sure your expectations of marriage are based in truth. Grieve the loss of the fantasy marriage so you can accept the reality of what you have. Seek God to fulfill you and heal you rather than expect your spouse to do what only God can do.

THINGS TO DO IF YOUR SPOUSE
Won't Stop Clinging to Unrealistic Expectations

- Be sure you are meeting whatever expectations are realistic rather than giving up altogether.

- If you performed a "bait and switch" and act in a completely different manner than you did while dating, admit this to your spouse and ask forgiveness.

- Seek counseling for both of you so a third party can define reality and realistic expectations.

- Develop a deeper understanding of the wound within your spouse that is driving his or her unrealistic expectations of you.

- Determine to grow in areas where you can.

- Be sure you are communicating about your spouse's disappointment and your continued desire to meet realistic needs.

- Determine that you will not allow disappointment to rule your mind because of your spouse's unrealistic expectations.

[STOP OBSESSING]
ON THE PAST

To watch a short video on this subject, go to
7MinuteMarriageSolution.com/2

On your honeymoon, were you amazed at how much emotional baggage showed up along with your luggage and travel gear? If so, you are not alone. The lack of clarity is one of the most common traits found in early marriages. And you are also not alone if you did not handle the reality of what you discovered very well. If your reactions to your spouse's emotional baggage made things worse rather than better, I have some hope to offer you.

ALL OF US BRING INTO MARRIAGE
THE RESIDUE FROM OUR PAST.

All of us bring into marriage the residue from our past. Many people carry emotional scars—and sometimes physical ones as well—from the harmful acts others inflicted on them. These traumas usually occur before courtship, and the victim brings them into the marriage as dark clouds that cast a shadow over the relationship.

Usually the person bearing these emotional shadows comes into the marriage thinking the painful event is buried so deeply that it no longer has any effect. But this is seldom true, especially if it has not been dealt with and resolved in some way. When this person marries, the intimacy of the marital relationship is likely to bring the effects of the past trauma to the surface—especially as the chemical reactions from romance wear off.

Quit Seeing Yourself as a Victim

When you marry a person bearing emotional pain, you can make things worse by looking only at the effect your mate's issue has on you personally. You can see yourself as a victim of your spouse's pain, regret your marriage, and look for a way out—or you can seek to understand the cause of the behavior and help your mate find healing. This is the choice my friend Cody had to face.

Shortly after Cody married, he found that his wife had hidden from him a dark shadow from her past. On their wedding night that shadow emerged and threatened to undo their relationship. Cody did not realize that Rhonda carried deep-seated psychological problems resulting from childhood sexual and physical abuse inflicted by her stepfather. These problems had remained more or less dormant until she entered the intimacy of marriage. During their dating period, Cody had interpreted Rhonda's lack of sexual interest as a sign of her strong faith. He did not know that sex was an area she would not and could not enter. Once married it became obvious that the abuse Rhonda had endured was so severe she found it impossible to trust anyone enough to allow a sexual relationship—even with her husband, Cody, whom she loved dearly.

Although Cody tried to be gentle and understanding, Rhonda's fears increased until she had to be confined in institutional psychiatric care. She was in the hospital much more than she was home with Cody. Even when she was home, she had to be supervised to prevent suicide attempts. At the time, the right medication for her particular pathology had not been developed.

When Cody married Rhonda, he did not expect to have to deal with such a deep and disturbing relational problem. Now he faced a hard choice: Either he could put Rhonda away as damaged goods and justify himself by saying, "This is not what I bought into. No man could be expected to put up with this, so no one will blame me if I get a divorce." Or he could stick by his vow to take this woman "for better or for worse" and work toward finding healing for her.

Rather than curse his fate or resent his wife for hiding her condition, which he could easily have done, Cody stood by Rhonda through her many long-term hospitalizations, remaining faithful and chaste all the while. He studied up on her condition, reading book after book, attending classes, and searching the Internet for relevant information. He learned how he should treat her and how to rebuild her trust in men. As a result, over a ten-year period, she regained normalcy and learned to trust Cody and love him deeply. With the help of newly formulated medication combined with the work she had done toward her own healing, she finally put institutionalization behind her completely. Today Cody and Rhonda have as happy a marriage as I have ever seen.

Cody did what my friend, pastoral counselor Milan Yerkovich, advises the mate of a wounded spouse to do: "The best strategy is to get a Ph.D. in the wounds of your spouse."[1] In other words, become an expert on your mate's hurts. Do all you can to uncover the underlying cause of the impaired behavior. Dig into it until you understand it, and then take steps to help your mate address and resolve the problem. This is what Cody did, and it bound his marriage together with real intimacy.

Cody's Christlike action turns the prevalent mind-set of today's culture upside down. Instead of seeing himself as a victim and getting rid of the woman who ruined his happiness and disappointed his expectations, he chose to stick by his vow and love her through her ordeal. He demonstrated that his love for his wife was not merely a superficial, "what's in it for me?" love. It was deeply compassionate love. The result was not only a healed wife and a happy marriage, but also an inspiring reflection of the God who loved and rescued us while we were yet sinners.

Understand Your Mate's Pain

Sensitivity to your mate's hurts means trying your best to understand what has happened to him or her in the past, as well as the effect those hurts have on the present. You build a strong connection between the other person's pain and your own understanding.

This commitment to understanding your mate's pain accomplishes three things: First, it does what we Christians are consistently enjoined to do—to separate the problem from the person. This separation allows you to hate and attack the problem without hating or attacking the person. You realize that the effects of the trauma your mate is carrying do not define who he or she is. You see your mate as a victim who bears the pain of evil inflicted. Just as physical pain often causes us to writhe and twist our bodies in an attempt to escape it, the agony of emotional pain causes us to writhe and twist in our inner selves, distorting our relationships and preventing intimacy.

IF YOU DON'T BUILD THIS BRIDGE TO THE PAST—
FROM WHERE YOU ARE NOW TO THE CAUSE OF
THE PAIN—YOU WILL NEVER TRULY KNOW YOUR
SPOUSE EVEN AFTER YEARS OF BEING TOGETHER.

Second, your commitment to understanding your mate's pain puts you in a position to establish a strong relational connection as you build a bridge of empathy. If you don't build this bridge to the past—from where you are now to the cause of the pain—you will never truly know your spouse even after years of being together. Part of him or her will be living in a place you can never go until you build that bridge.

Third, seeing your mate as the victim of events instead of as the perpetrator of the effects enables you to accept and forgive more easily. When the pain of your mate's past spills over into actions that hurt you, your understanding allows you to bear that hurt without anger or resentment because you understand the real source of it. You see those hurtful actions not as personal attacks but for what they are—the spill-off from a debilitating weight of pain the other has borne for perhaps many years. This more accurate viewpoint makes an offense much easier to forgive.

When Don was a child, his father spanked him to the point of inflicting bruises for the slightest infraction of the rules his dad imposed on his family. After each beating, Don's sympathetic mother would sneak cookies or cake to him as compensation for what he endured. Thus Don developed the habit of using food to relieve the tension of stressful situations.

Don married Sherry, a health-conscious woman who regularly prepared nutritious meals. When Don began to gain weight, Sherry suspected he was sneaking unhealthy food behind her back. She found evidence of it and confronted him. He denied the charge, and the guilt brought on by his lying caused him to withdraw emotionally from her. Sherry was hurt by his withdrawal, but because she was able to see the effect of the past on Don's present actions, she could forgive the emotional pain Don was inflicting on her. She understood its source.

Sherry sought help through her church's counseling ministry. Don, though reluctant, finally agreed to go. In time his reluctance eased away as he began to see the benefits and decided to follow the counselor's program. Though it was difficult at first and punctuated with several slips, he eventually won victory over his food addiction, which restored trust and intimacy with Sherry.

Sherry found it easy to love Don through the trying times of his emotional withdrawal because she could see that his secret eating was caused by a problem that was inflicted on him by others in his past. An added bonus for her efforts is that he now has a healthy physique!

In these situations, when pain was inflicted on your spouse by someone else, you can start to resent the fact that your spouse did not disclose this pain or attempt to resolve it before marriage. Either way, you need to stop obsessing on the past. Instead of dwelling on your spouse's emotional baggage and viewing yourself as a victim of his or her pain, extend grace to your spouse. You can be a healing force in your spouse's life, even if he or she has waited to initiate healing.

Not all of the pain you experience is going to be a result of someone else hurting your spouse. Your spouse is going to do some things that hurt you. Some of those will be extremely painful. But I can tell you from my own experience that when you work through those hurts and resolve them in a godly and healthy way, they will lead you to a deeper connection than you ever thought possible. So when your spouse hurts you, you can give up—or you can dig deep and find the compassionate love and grace that is required for two imperfect people to love each other forever.

Dealing with Hurt from Your Mate's Sexual Past

In today's anything-goes sexual climate, you wouldn't think past sexual experiences could damage a marriage. It would seem that so many people today bring a sexual history into marriage that its presence would be generally assumed and accepted. Don't misunderstand me: I am not justifying today's sexual license; I am merely recognizing the reality of it. But the reality does not reduce the negative effects. In my helping couples transform their marriages I have found that past sexual experience can damage a married relationship in several ways.

Roger and Carolyn had been married three years when a friend dropped a hint about Carolyn's sexual past. The couple had never discussed their sexual history, and Roger had assumed Carolyn to be as virginal as he was. When he confronted her, she admitted that she had been a little wild in her college days, engaging in several one-night stands and three or four sexual relationships lasting a few months each.

Roger was stunned. He could not cope with the revelation, and imaginary visions of Carolyn's sexual encounters haunted him continually. He became angry, depressed, and could no longer bring himself to have sex with her, fearing that she would compare him to her more experienced partners of the past. When he suggested divorce, Carolyn insisted they seek counseling first.

Counseling helped Roger understand that everyone comes into a relationship with baggage from the past, whether sexual or otherwise. Everyone has done things they are sorry for and wish had never occurred. Carolyn was not proud of her past, but it had nothing to do with Roger since he did not know her then. And when they did marry, she was not the same person she had been in her past. In fact, she had married Roger because he was so different from other men who were interested only in her body. When they were dating, Roger had surprised her by not pushing her into sex because he respected her and loved her for who she was. He did not sleep around because he had integrity and valued commitment. Before they married she felt secure in the relationship. The feeling of security and those strong character qualities attracted Carolyn and made her see the shallowness of casual sex indulged for superficial pleasure. She felt clean and whole with Roger. And she came to love him as she had never loved anyone.

Did Roger want to throw away their marriage because of something that had happened long ago? Something his wife could not go back and change even though she herself had changed? Did he want to undo their vows and start over with another woman who would bring a whole new set of past experiences into the relationship? He asked himself these questions rather than do what many would do in the same situation: use his spouse's past to pull away, reject, and isolate.

When people who have been sexually active in the past get married, problems often arise. These problems may be more acute when a person who has been sexually active marries a person who has not, as in Roger and Carolyn's case. The inexperienced partner can feel haunted by a sense of inadequacy due to his lack of experience in the face of his partner's wide experience. He can feel that his wife is comparing his performance with her past sexual partners, and he may wonder whether he is satisfying her as well as they did. He can feel that she has shared intimate parts of herself with others that should belong only to him.

A corresponding problem in some cases can be that such fears are real. A sexually experienced partner who is focused heavily on receiving sexual pleasure may indeed compare and think he or she has known better sexual partners, causing disappointment in the mate and regret over marrying this particular person.

These problems can emerge even in marriages where both partners have past sexual experiences. Feelings of jealousy or resentment can boil up when one imagines—or perhaps even has reason to believe—those past liaisons linger in the other's mind. Another common problem arising from past sexual activity is the guilt either or both can feel over past sexual sins. That guilt can intrude on the relationship in the form of sexual dysfunctions or withdrawal from intimacy.

Perhaps the biggest problem that can arise out of one's sexual past is what Roger experienced with Carolyn: the shock of discovery when a partner's hidden past is unexpectedly revealed.

Due to the differences in people's psyches, there is no one-size-fits-all way to deal with these shadows from the past. The best way, of course, is not to indulge in premarital sex at all. But given the fact that the majority of the people who marry today carry a sexual past with them, we must face that reality and deal with what is rather than what should be.

The best way for couples to deal with past sexual experiences, as with all past mistakes and sins, is to be honest with each other before they marry. Openness and transparency is a key to intimacy, and by revealing and confessing your past mistakes before the wedding, you show your mate that you are hiding nothing and that you want everything out in the open. You want no secrets to emerge later that would cause the other to regret the marriage. You clear the air before you breathe it in to say "I do." In so doing you intensify the clarity you need to build the relationship.

Couples who do not confess their sexual sins before marriage often find that there is a need to do it afterward when one or more of the problems outlined above emerge. Revelation after the marriage has the disadvantage of showing that you have hidden something from your mate, and it will add to the issues of honesty, trust, and security.

Whether this openness about your sexual history occurs before or after the marriage, you need to be willing to offer your partner as much or as little information as he or she wants to know. In some cases, the partner may want to hear only the outlines of your past, and the details are unimportant. Others may have more trouble dealing with their mate's past, as Roger did, and need more in-depth information, painful though it is. If he doesn't hear the details, he is likely to imagine them; but hearing them from you may cause him to relive them over and over in his head. You can provide full and complete disclosure without revealing every detail.

Withholding details may be more comfortable for you and less painful for your mate, but anything you refuse to tell may be interpreted as closing the door in his face to some part of your life that you have shared with another but will not share with him. It is sure to create distance. Of course, when you do reveal those details, you run another risk: your mate may reject you because he cannot handle the revelation. There's no way around it—sin creates problems, and often there are no easy ways to resolve them. Yet the attempt must be made, and if two partners want to save the marriage, they can find a way.

If your mate presses you for something you are reticent to tell because revealing it will cause pain either to you or to him, you might say, "I'll tell you this if you really want me to, but I have put it in the past and have no need to go there ever again. The person I once was is dead now. If you can let it lie where it is, I think it would be better for both of us. But if you feel that you must hear it in order to deal with it, I will tell you if you insist." It's a risk you have to take.

When such revelations occur, couples should be prepared for certain pitfalls they may face in the process. If you are the partner hearing your spouse's revelation, you must be prepared to bear the pain of things you won't like to hear. It may hurt more deeply than you anticipate to learn that your spouse has shared the most intimate parts of herself with others— parts that you feel should be reserved only for you. You may feel that your mate's past sexual partners have stolen something valuable from you. For this reason, it's best that you ask only for what details you are prepared to hear and can deal with.

If you are the partner revealing your sexual past to your mate, it is good to accompany the revelation with confession. You need to recognize and admit that what you did was wrong. You need to say that you are ashamed of your mistake and that you are committed never to do it again. The past is behind you. You have buried it and you never dig it up to cling to it or wish you could have it back. God has forgiven you, and you beg your mate to forgive you too. You also need to assure your mate that he or she is now your only love, your whole life. You are committed totally to your marriage and to your future together.

On receiving a confession of past sexual sins, the other mate completes the reconciliation and healing of the relationship by forgiving. Forgiveness may not be easy, and it may be necessary for your mate to absorb the information and work through his or her own hurt and shock before coming to a place where forgiveness can occur cleanly. I will deal more fully with forgiveness and all it entails in chapter 10.

Once past sexual sins are brought into the open and dealt with, I recommend that, as with all sins that have been repented of and forgiven, you never bring them up again.

Dealing with Past Issues within the Marriage

Not all hurts of the past occur before marriage. Married partners can develop an immense capacity for inflicting severe and debilitating wounds on each other. And these hurts can linger and eat away at the relationship if they are not dealt with effectively.

Some examples of hurts within a marriage are obvious, such as adultery, abuse, abandonment, or addictions. These are serious issues, and we will deal with them later in this book. But in this chapter, we are focusing on past mistakes or choices in the marriage that are not as severe as the four deadly A's—choices such as broken promises, failure to support one's mate emotionally, deception, misuse of money, or making solo decisions. Acts such as these inflict pain that can cause lingering resentment or regret and loosen the bonds of marriage.

The effect of a hurt from your spouse within the marriage can be worse than one inflicted by someone else before the marriage. It involves a breach of trust because it comes from a source from which only love should flow. This can drive the pain deeper and make repair more difficult. But these mate-inflicted hurts need not destroy a marriage. If the isues are handled carefully, the marriage can actually come out stronger after the hurt is addressed and healed.

Dennis and Gail had been married six years and had two children when Gail discovered that he had lied to her. He had told her he was taking a company trip to another state, but instead he slipped off with his buddies for a three-day fishing trip in the mountains. Dennis admitted it, repented of his deception, and vowed never to lie to her again. But Gail no longer trusted him. She pulled away emotionally, and though they maintained the appearance of a good marriage, the distance between them grew. Dennis tried his best to restore trust and intimacy, but Gail simply could not get over the hurt. Her reaction caused Dennis to become angry and impatient with her, and their relationship deteriorated further.

Up to a point, the healing process in a case like this is the same as for healing past offenses inflicted by others: First, the offended mate must develop objectivity and empathy by looking beneath the surface to detect and understand the underlying cause of the offense. Could it be that one had done something in the past that caused the other's offending behavior?

Counseling helped Dennis and Gail to look beneath the surface of the problem. Under the counselor's guidance, Gail saw that since the children arrived, all the care and attention she had previously lavished on Dennis was now directed toward the children. Dennis, thinking only of himself, had turned to his fishing buddies for companionship. This did not excuse his lie, but it allowed her to understand the dynamic that had set it up. She also realized Dennis could have done worse; he could have turned to another woman instead of to his buddies.

This kind of objectivity is not easy when you are the one who has been hurt. But it can be achieved if someone has the incredible willingness that Gail possessed. Again, it's the principle of separating the sin from the sinner, which is one of the requirements of Christian forgiveness.

Counseling showed both Dennis and Gail the effective steps to restoring trust and intimacy. Dennis learned that his impatience was misplaced.

He was the guilty party, and though he tried to restore trust by being truthful, it took time for his trustworthiness to be proven to Gail.

The counselor urged Gail to forgive Dennis, accept him back fully, and restore intimacy with him. But forgiveness is a process. She was willing to see the situation from both sides, but she was not so sure about rushing in with forgiveness with the risk that he might turn around and do the same thing again. She wondered how to know if he could be trusted.

YOU CAN NEVER KNOW WHAT A PERSON
IS GOING TO DO IN THE FUTURE.
TRUST ALWAYS INVOLVES RISK.

The answer is, you can't know. You can never know what a person is going to do in the future. Trust always involves risk. One good way to reduce the risk is for the couple to agree to boundaries that will help assure the offended mate that a repetition of the offense is unlikely. In the case of Roger and Gail, he promised to show her his airline tickets and hotel reservations when he took a trip on company business in the future. He would always give her a landline number where he could be reached.

Even with good boundaries in place, we are still flawed creatures who fail occasionally. But we cannot find happiness by closing off relationships because of that universal failing. We must plunge in and trust and love and forgive with no absolute certainty that we will never be hurt again. It is the only way to restore a relationship and the only way to have a strong marriage.

That is not the same as excusing a repeat offender. There is a time for forgiveness and there is a time for action. If you are being repeatedly betrayed you must not push toward forgiveness before you have done all you can to confront the behavior, demand change, and require help that will cause the pattern of betrayal to be broken. The rush to forgiveness is an easy temptation. But it can become an act of enabling evil. The evil must stop before forgiveness is appropriate. Proverbs 10:10 tells us that to wink at wrong—in other words, to minimize how severe a problem is or to just let it go—brings trouble. An open rebuke, or confronting and talking about the reality that is before us and taking action based on truth, can lead to a lasting peace because it resolves the problem at hand rather than allowing it to enlarge. We are never to minimize or deny that the evil is there. Often the bold move that is required to help the situation is ignored and the situation gets worse rather than better. That is enabling evil.

There are a lot of things you can do in response to your spouse's past, but the most destructive choice you can make in the face of a repentant offender is to hold the past against him or her. The best choice is born out of love. Love is the one indispensable key to healing past hurts. You can find healing if you love enough to work through the hurt and restore your relationship. Your marriage will be the stronger for it.

7

THINGS TO DO IF YOUR SPOUSE
Won't Stop Obsessing on Your Past

- Be sure that you are truly repentant and not involved in an ongoing pattern of betrayal.

- Ask your mate what you can do to make restitution to make things right.

- Continue to ask for forgiveness and be willing to discuss the past until there is no longer a need to talk about the offense.

- Set up safeguards and protections that ensure the past mistake won't happen again.

- Get help for that particular vulnerability by attending counseling.

- Select two or three friends (of the same sex) to be your accountability partners for this particular issue. Meet weekly with them, and be willing to answer their questions honestly.

- Participate in a character-building process such as a Bible study that shows how determined you are that the problem not be repeated and that you continue to grow from it.

[STOP DROWNING]
IN SUSPICION AND JEALOUSY

To watch a short video on this subject, go to
7MinuteMarriageSolution.com/3

As I write this chapter, a television commercial airing for an insurance company stresses that its agents are always there for you, day or night. It features a husband alone in his home, talking quietly on the phone late at night. His suspicious wife, thinking she's caught him red-handed, strides angrily into the room and demands to know who he's talking to. He replies that it's Jake from State Farm. Not believing him, she snatches the phone, thrusts it to her ear, and says sarcastically, "Well, Jake from State Farm, what are you wearing?" The scene switches to the agent's office where Jake sits, phone in hand. Nonplussed by the strange question, he says, "Uh, khakis."

The commercial makes us laugh, but there's nothing funny about spousal suspicion and the jealousy that drives it. Suspicion and jealousy can be vicious and destructive, leading to oppressive control and even abusive behavior. It can turn a spouse into a tenacious watchdog tracking all the moves and activities of the other. It can mean police-like grilling for all details as to where a spouse went and what that spouse did. It can show itself in frequent phone calls to be sure the spouse is where he or she claims to be. It often involves monitoring phone calls and every other source of connection. It drives controlling and demeaning actions.

We can understand the suspicion of the wife in the insurance commercial. It was late at night and her husband was in another room on the phone, talking low. As it turned out, he was innocent. In many cases, the suspicion in a marriage is unfounded. The suspicious and jealous spouse merely interprets normal events in the worst possible way rather than believing the best about the spouse.

That's how it was with Margie. She suspected her husband, Jeff, of running around on her every time he came home late from work. She was suspicious when he went on a business trip with his boss, fishing with his buddies, or even when he dined with a male client at a restaurant. The truth was, Jeff was completely faithful to Margie. The suspicion problem was rooted in her past and not in Jeff's actions.

Margie was raised in a home where distrust was a way of life. Her father was unfaithful to her mother and exhibited secretive behavior that caused her mother's distrust to grow. Following the pattern of her mother, Margie regularly checked her husband's whereabouts, his computer files, and his cell phone, seeking verification of the activities he reported. She never found anything wrong, but her suspicions destroyed any chance for intimacy with her husband. In reality Jeff was a faithful guy who loved her. But he grew more and more distant with each false accusation.

Finally Jeff told Margie she must get help or he was moving out. He didn't want to move out; he wanted her to get help. And she did. The counseling revealed much to her. It soon became apparent that the source of her problem was her father's continual unfaithfulness during her younger years. She thought her dad was the most immoral man she had ever known—that is, until the pastor she went to for counseling years ago approached her sexually.

To Margie, therefore, it was "normal" for men to be untrustworthy and for wives to be suspicious. She expected her husband to act like her father, and that triggered her to act like her mother, doing surveillance instead of trusting him.

Too often a problem in our marriage is an unresolved experience from our past. Someone did not give us what we needed, and now our desire for it is so intense and out of balance that the people in our lives today cannot provide it or compensate for it. We place unrealistic demands on people, and the result is disconnection and disruption of the relationship. It is a call for us to look back—not to dwell on the past, but to see if the past has any connection to our present problems.

Scripture tells us to throw off anything that might get in the way of our moving toward the finish line (Hebrews 12:1). If the past is controlling the present, it needs to be dealt with, resolved, and healed.

When Suspicion Is Justified

Sometimes the marriage partner is not acting innocently and the suspicion is justified. In this case, you need to be objective about the behavior of your mate. When you see real signs of furtive behavior, deception, or secretiveness, don't ignore them. Insist on mutual accountability where behavior could arouse suspicion and distrust.

Certain behaviors naturally arouse distrust, such as a mate spending an inordinate amount of time away that he or she cannot adequately account for. A mate who stays up late every night alone at the computer should raise a flag. If a mate refuses to share computer passwords or engages in secretive behavior, that's suspicious. If one mate walks into the room when the other is talking to someone else and the conversation suddenly ceases, that's suspicious. Or if one walks into the room and the other immediately clicks off the phone or the website, there may be reason for distrust.

My friend and *New Life Live* cohost psychologist John Townsend tells of an incident in which Vicky's friend tells her that she has just seen Alex, Vicky's husband, lunching at a restaurant with an old girlfriend. Dr. Townsend writes, "When Vicky asked why he hadn't mentioned it to her, his reply was defensive: 'I knew you would freak out, like you're doing now.'"[1] Alex had no business opening up his life to an old girlfriend at a lunch where they would be alone. By not disclosing the meeting to his wife, he showed that his intentions were wrong from the beginning. The old girlfriend needed to be either completely out of his life or part of the life he shared with his wife.

I don't know of any situation where it is appropriate for a man to meet with an old girlfriend without his wife's presence. That is messing around with marital dynamite. A high number of affairs begin when old flames get in touch later in life. It's a good thing for married couples to trust each other, but it's important to trust only what it makes sense to trust. Your mate eating out with someone of the opposite sex without you does not make good sense at all. Anyone thinking otherwise has probably not been burned by a budding affair that started at a meeting away from the other spouse.

By far the worst breach of trust in any marriage is unfaithfulness. Statistics on infidelity are notoriously undependable, and it's easy to understand why. The guilty parties are not likely to be open about it. But according to one survey, one-fourth of all marriages in America experience physical infidelity on the part of at least one partner. The figure jumps to 41 percent when both emotional and physical infidelity are included.[2] Statistics from other sources list percentages ranging from 30 to 60 percent.

In spite of these variations in data, almost all statisticians agree on two things: First, the incidence of marital infidelity is steadily increasing, and second, infidelity has become almost as prevalent in women as in men. Undoubtedly these facts contribute to the increasing rate of divorce. In fact, a mere 31 percent of marriages last after an affair has been admitted or discovered.[3]

There are many reasons for the increase in infidelity, and each of them gives couples more reason for suspicion. E-mail, Internet chat rooms, and social media such as Facebook make it easier to begin and maintain secretive relationships, as do the sexes mixing freely in the workplace and educational facilities. Thirty-six percent of extramarital affairs begin in the workplace or on business trips.[4] No doubt the obsessive cultural emphasis on sex and the right to sexual satisfaction also contributes to the problem.

While infidelity is an enormous breach of trust, it does not have to end a marriage. There are excellent reasons for mates reeling from infidelity to do the painful work of rebuilding trust and holding the marriage together. There are a number of ways in which this can be done.

Trust in marriage can be damaged or lost in many other ways, both small and large. An obvious one is lack of truthfulness or outright lying.

Similarly, when one mate attempts to hide habits, activities, or even private addictions from the other, it's a cause for distrust. Mates should be able to trust each other with their deepest secrets in total confidence.

> IF DISTRUST EXISTS IN YOUR MARRIAGE,
> BEGIN NOW TO TAKE POSITIVE STEPS TO
> UNCOVER THE CAUSES AND THEN WORK
> ON THOSE ISSUES TO REBUILD TRUST.

As Jesus said in Matthew 12:25, a "house divided against itself will not stand" (NKJV). Failure to trust or to earn trust leaves your house divided and in danger of falling. If distrust exists in your marriage, begin now to take positive steps to uncover the causes and then work on those issues to rebuild trust. That may mean either confronting your mate or digging painfully into your own soul to determine what you are doing to cause distrust. In either case, it means taking responsibility to correct the issue and rebuild trust.

Rebuilding Your Marriage on Trust

In the last years of the nineteenth century, Buffalo Bill's Wild West Show was a traveling show that provided all the excitement and thrills of the modern-day Cirque du Soleil. One of its most popular events was the petite sharpshooter Annie Oakley. She could aim her rifle and hit a playing card edgewise from a distance of ninety feet.

Buffalo Bill took Annie to Europe with his show in the summer of 1897. At one performance Annie completed a series of spectacular shots and then called for a volunteer from the audience to hold a lit cigarette in his mouth while she shot the ashes off the end of it. To the surprise of everyone, who should volunteer but the German prince, Wilhelm II. The shot was successful with no harmful effects—other than the need for the prince to relight his cigarette.[5]

Obviously Wilhelm trusted Annie Oakley's shooting ability. It was not blind trust, because in watching her show he had seen her perform every shot successfully. Based on this evidence, he trusted her so completely that he was willing to put his life in her hands, at least for that one shot.

The expertise of people like Annie Oakley amazes me, but I'm not sure I could muster up the kind of trust required to put my life in her hands. (Okay, I'm sure I could *not* muster up that kind of trust.) Yet when it came to marriage, I did muster it up. I trusted my well-being, my life, and a major part of my happiness to my wife. And amazingly, she did the same with me. On that day when the minister stood before us and asked if she would love and honor and give herself to me from that moment until the day death separates us, she placed enormous trust in me. She trusted me to love her, protect her, support her, and treat her honorably and respectfully.

The trust my wife and I have for each other is not blind trust. Just as Wilhelm II trusted Annie Oakley because he had witnessed her sharpshooting accuracy, my wife and I trust each other because we have seen trustworthiness demonstrated in each other. If, when we were dating, I had failed to show up for dates or arrived consistently late or made promises I didn't keep, she would rightly have been reluctant to trust me. Or if after our relationship became serious I had flirted with or ogled other women, she would have known I was untrustworthy and severed the relationship.

There is another reason we have built trust in each other. Misty and I both brought children into this marriage from previous marriages. We knew that blended and blessed families are rare. So before we married, we agreed to give each other a lot of grace over our past and to extend a lot of grace toward each other's children. When she saw me earn the respect of her boys rather than demand it, it built her trust in me. When I saw her make allowances for my child that met her unique needs, I knew I could trust her. Both of us acted consistently with our promises.

You have heard that love is blind, but it shouldn't be. If you find yourself in danger of falling in love with someone who breaches your trust, you had better open your eyes, see the handwriting on the wall, and break off the relationship before trapping yourself for a lifetime. The breaches of trust that you see before marriage will not suddenly change just because you say "I do."

Couples build trust by being trustworthy. Yet even when a potential mate has proven trustworthy, plunging into marriage still involves risk. There's no way around it; in this fallen world, trust involves risk.

Your potential partner may pass every reasonable test of trust, but in the uncharted seas of marriage you will encounter unanticipated shoals and currents that can cause trust to founder. The joys of marriage make the risk worthwhile, however. The best marriages are those in which each spouse takes care to build trust and then acts to preserve trust and repair it when it is breached.

Build Trust by Guarding Your Relationship

As I have already noted, a spouse's relationships with members of the opposite sex can raise trust issues in a marriage. Many people today work in offices that place them in regular contact with members of the other sex. Friendships may develop in meetings or when working in adjacent cubicles or on mutual projects. In a marriage where the bond is strong and trust prevails, these harmless opposite-sex friendships usually raise no cause for alarm. But situations can arise that threaten trust and lead to suspicion or jealousy, as the following story shows.

As head of the art department for a major book publisher, Derek and the company production manager often flew to printing plants to check the color accuracy of projects on the press. The trips usually took three or four days. When the publisher hired a woman as the new production manager, Derek told his wife, Amy, that the two of them would be scheduled to take these trips together.

Even though Amy knew Derek was a strong Christian and had always been a faithful husband, the situation bothered her for several reasons: First, she felt that a man and woman taking repeated trips together for three or four days, sharing flights, meals, work, and even staying in the same hotel could create undue temptation, even for morally upright people. And she was absolutely right. Even the strongest Christian should never allow such an arrangement. Second, even if nothing immoral occurred, the trips could cause ugly rumors, damaging Derek's reputation. Third, although she trusted Derek, she did not know whether the woman was morally trustworthy.

Derek's response to Amy's concerns could either strengthen or damage her trust in him. He could have been affronted by Amy's reaction. He could have insisted that her concerns indicated a lack of trust in him. After all, he had proved his commitment and faithfulness through two decades of marriage. He could have asserted that it was all in her head—her problem, not his.

But that is not what Derek did. He put himself in Amy's shoes and made the right choice—the smart choice. What if she was the one flying on four-day trips with a man? He trusted Amy, but he wouldn't like it. Looking at the situation from her point of view made him see that such an arrangement was loaded with danger. So he understood Amy's concerns. He also knew that even committed Christians with strong moral integrity are not immune to temptation. He remembered Paul's warning in 1 Corinthians 10:12: "If you think you are standing firm, be careful that you don't fall!" (NIV).

Derek candidly expressed his concern to his vice president and convinced him that two people were not needed to check printing on the press. The woman's business with the printer was solely bids and pricing, and that could be done on separate trips. The VP agreed and the problem was solved.

But what if the VP had ruled the other way and insisted that the two travel together? Derek had already determined what he would do: he had promised Amy beforehand that in such a case, he would ask for reassignment or resign. To Derek and Amy, maintaining trust in their marriage was more important than his career. But beyond trust, Derek was ensuring that his sexual integrity and deep connection would remain intact.

One of the best ways for people of integrity to protect trust in their marriage is to set rules and guidelines, as Derek did, that will help them avoid any appearance of wrongdoing. Wise pastors and other counselors usually observe certain protective rules. Some pastors, for example, will counsel women only when other people are in the building, and they will not close their office door while the counseling is in session. Doctors, who must at times see and touch the opposite sex in intimate places, have guidelines that require the presence of another medical professional, usually a nurse, in the examining room. I encourage married people not to dine one-on-one with the opposite sex or ride with them in a vehicle without a third passenger.

YOUR WILLINGNESS TO TAKE FIRM STEPS TO
MAINTAIN TRUST SPEAKS VOLUMES, MAKING YOUR
MATE FEEL HIGHLY VALUED AND PROTECTED.

Some of these rules may seem overly puritanical in today's social climate. But at times Christians must ignore popular opinion and swim against the current in order to show they are serious about purity, marital fidelity, and especially the feelings of their mates. Even if your peers scorn such guidelines, you can be sure your spouse will appreciate them. It's a way of earning and maintaining trust. Your willingness to take firm steps to maintain trust speaks volumes, making your mate feel highly valued and protected.

Banish Suspicion and Jealousy by Earning Trust

"One of the most wonderful gifts of a loving marriage is the ability to trust your mate," writes John Townsend.[6] He goes on to describe some of the characteristics of trust. It means you and your mate are the same person on the inside as on the outside. Trust means both of you have the best interests of the other at heart. Both keep your promises. Both are open and transparent with each other. These attributes create an atmosphere of safety and security, and they promote a deeper capacity to love because they enhance the clarity and security priorities in the relationship.

I really like what Dr. Townsend says next: "One of the Old Testament words for trust (*batach*) has a meaning of 'careless.' Think about it: When you trust your spouse, you feel so safe that you are careless—or free of concern—with him or her. You don't have to hide who you are or to be self-protective."[7] Of course, Dr. Townsend isn't speaking of *carelessness* in the way we generally use it, which means being irresponsible. He means "care-less" as in without a need to take undue care and caution around your mate. You don't have to be wary or defensive. It means being free of any fear that would cause you to hold back from the other any part of yourself. When your trust is "care-less," you give yourself to your mate with total abandon and produce a deep serenity in the marriage.

That kind of "care-less" oneness doesn't just happen; it has to be earned. It has to be built layer by layer into the relationship. It starts while you are courting, but it must continue throughout the entire marriage. It is the key element of marital clarity and security.

THINGS TO DO IF YOUR SPOUSE
Won't Stop Drowning in Suspicion and Jealousy

- Determine to be the most predictable spouse on the planet.
- Inform your spouse of any change of plans.
- Make all sources of communication and connection open for your spouse's review.
- Eradicate any secrecy from your behavior.
- Point out all you have done to reassure your spouse of your trustworthiness and ask him or her to get some help in dealing with the insecurities that remain. Be willing to go to counseling with your spouse.
- If the jealousy or suspicion is a result of recent betrayal, do not expect trust to be regained quickly. Give your spouse time, and understand his or her need to know where you are and who you are with at any time until trust can be reestablished.
- Continue to reassure your spouse of your love in as many ways as possible.

4

[STOP TRYING]

TO CHANGE YOUR MATE

To watch a short video on this subject, go to
7MinuteMarriageSolution.com/4

Ever try to fix a broken lawn mower with a waffle iron? A foolish thought, isn't it? The waffle iron is a fabulous tool when it comes to making waffles. But try to use it for lawn mower repair, and it quickly becomes evident it is the wrong tool. Screwdrivers and box wrenches are much better, though they can't make a waffle worth pouring syrup over. A tool that works well at one thing would be an absolute disaster at something else. You are like a waffle iron. You are an amazing tool for creating a lot of wonderful things in this world. But when it comes to fixing your spouse, you are the wrong tool. You can't do it. So it is time to stop trying.

Vivian loved Robert, but in public she was ashamed of him. They had met and married when she was in college. He didn't go to college, but he owned and ran a farm supply franchise and did quite well at it.

Vivian was now a professor and had published a couple of reasonably successful books. She was often invited to dinners and receptions, and on these occasions she found herself embarrassed by her husband's unsophisticated conversation. Neither his vocabulary nor his clothing was quite up to the level of her academic peers.

So, like Professor Henry Higgins in *My Fair Lady*, Vivian undertook the task of remaking her blue-collar husband into a refined gentleman. She began to correct his grammar and his mispronounced words. She also began to suggest the kinds of clothing he should buy, and she let him know when any of his present clothing seemed a little too redneckish.

Naturally, the continued criticism of his speech and dress irritated Robert, and he told her so. "I'm just trying to help you," Vivian explained. "I'm offering a little constructive criticism."

Robert understood what was going on: his wife disapproved of him, and he resented it. When he resisted her makeover attempt, Vivian stopped asking him to accompany her to dinners and receptions. She could not accept him for the simple, working guy he was.

I have seen it happen many times. A woman envisions her husband as a reconstruction project. She sees him as raw material for her expert shaping. She makes it her calling to clean him up, chip away at his flaws, point him in a new direction, inject a dose of ambition, and reshape him into her ideal of what a husband should be.

Someone has said that a man marries a woman hoping she won't change, but she does. A woman marries a man hoping he will change, but he doesn't. The obvious solution in the face of these disappointments is to put your spouse on the anvil and beat him into shape. And it's not just a woman thing; both sexes are guilty of trying to change their mates. Husbands often attempt a similar transformation with their wives, trying to remake her into a Stepford wife or an avid sports fan or a fireball in the bedroom.

MAKEOVERS MAY WORK WONDERFULLY ON TV PROGRAMS, BUT NOT IN MARRIAGES.

Makeovers may work wonderfully on TV programs, but not in marriages. If you are trying to correct flaws in your husband or wife, you need to stop. Trying to change your mate will put distance between the two of you. The person you married came gift wrapped as a total package of mixed attributes. You knew much about what was in that package before you married, and on the whole, you liked what you knew or you wouldn't have married.

No doubt you knew the package contained a few things that didn't quite fit your tastes. But hopefully you came into the marriage prepared to accept those things instead of fixing them.

Of course, after you married, you found other less-than-attractive attributes you had not suspected. Most of these were well hidden before the wedding, so you may think you have a right to tackle anything you disapprove of and do something about it, right?

Wrong. You have no right—and really no power—to change that package. You didn't marry a lump of clay that is yours to mold into whatever shape pleases you. You committed to the package as is. Your responsibility—and the only way to make any marriage work—is to learn to live with your spouse and be happy. In this fallen world it is impossible to find a mate without flaws. And it is impossible for all our flaws to be eradicated in a lifetime. If you expect to have a spouse, you must prepare yourself to live with an imperfect one.

Please understand that when I speak of accepting flaws, I do not include abusive, adulterous, or abandonment situations. I would never encourage anyone to endure abuse or betrayal rather than get help when the spouse has crossed a destructive line. (I'll have more to say about this later.)

Who wants to spend a lifetime with a person who constantly corrects, criticizes, or judges you? You naturally prefer to be with someone who appreciates you for who you are and enjoys you without disapproval.

Putting Up with Your Mate's Annoying Behaviors

You may wonder about all I've said so far. "What am I supposed to do when my mate's behavior is annoying or repelling? Am I supposed to just let it go and ignore it?"

It all depends on the fault or the behavior. Most of your mate's flaws and weaknesses are not likely to be deep enough to warrant a change. These attributes may be annoying or unattractive, but you need to adjust to them and love your mate anyway. One helpful way to accept those flaws is to remind yourself that you would rather have this person in your life with the flaw than not to have him or her at all. This is a lesson Teresa learned—almost the hard way.

Teresa married Roy, a construction worker who handled all kinds of building materials and heavy tools. As a result, his hands were rough and calloused. In their lovemaking she could hardly stand the feel of his coarse hands moving across her skin like sandpaper. She nagged him continually to use lotion on his hands and wear gloves at work. But nothing worked. In time Roy's hands and Teresa's complaints took their toll, and the frequency of their lovemaking dropped to almost zero.

Then one day the news reported a serious accident at the construction site where Roy worked. Several men had been killed. Trembling with fear, Teresa called his boss's cell phone and learned that Roy was among the missing. *Please, God, don't let it be Roy—please!* After an hour of praying in utter agony, she got news that Roy had been taken to the hospital and released. He was okay.

That evening when he came in the door, Teresa threw her arms around his neck and showered him with kisses like never before. Then she took his calloused hands and kissed them tenderly. In bed that night she urged those hands to roam over her body anywhere they pleased. She never again complained, for to her the feel of Roy's sandpaper hands had become a touch of heaven.

Avoid Becoming the "Fixer"

We tend to take our wedding vows too lightly. When you married you stood at the *altar*, not the *alter*. When you promised to take the person beside you "for better or for worse," you made a solemn vow before God. You took on your partner's flaws, weaknesses, irritations, and all. Now your duty is to live up to your promise—not reluctantly with distaste or disapproval, but with full acceptance of the person you married for what he or she is.

When one mate assumes the right to fix the other, the result is ineffective at best and usually creates distance. Marriage is a bonding of equals. When one assumes the right to fix the other, the mutuality of the relationship goes out of balance and the marriage wobbles on its axis. The "fixer" assumes a superior position over the "fixee." The fixer becomes the judge and the fixee becomes the accused.

This imbalance generates negative emotions in both partners. The spouse on the receiving end of the fix feels resentment, rejection, and probably a sense of inadequacy. The spouse administering the fix exudes a sense of disapproval, and when the other mate resists the fix, that disapproval can expand into a grudge—an embedded offense that poisons every interaction between them.

The Poison of Criticism and Judgment

Most attempts at fixing a mate involve a program of criticism and judging—actions that build resistance and resentment. Criticism is the opposite of acceptance, which is why it has no place in your marriage. "Constructive" criticism is no better; it's nothing more than the same old criticism with a smile. Criticism of any kind is the opposite of acceptance, and its continued use destroys intimacy and builds walls.

And don't try to camouflage your criticism as advice. Unsolicited advice comes from the same bag of unworkable tricks as criticism.

The other negative element involved in trying to change your mate is judging. In a mutual relationship based on equality, how can one partner assume the position of judge over the other? What right has one partner to decide which standard should be used to determine whether a behavior is unacceptable and should be changed?

Please don't misunderstand me here. I am not advocating the postmodern idea that there are no standards of right and wrong except those we choose personally for ourselves. To the contrary, I strongly believe that right and wrong are firmly fixed absolutes that apply universally to everyone. My point is that in a marriage, one partner cannot assume the right to interpret and enforce what behaviors fall below that absolute standard. I am merely saying that one partner cannot be objective enough to be the judge and enforcer of the rules.

If at the end of a criminal trial, the prosecuting attorney went up to the bench, dumped the judge from his chair, picked up the gavel, and rendered a verdict of guilty, you might expect the defense attorney to object. A participant in the trial cannot also be the judge. You might suspect his judgment to be biased. None of us judges our own situation objectively.

A judgmental spouse also impairs a marriage in another way. Judging tends to expand from the particular to the general. Rather than limiting condemnation to a single, isolated flaw, judging makes a blanket assumption about the whole person based on that one flaw. Here's an example: Though both spouses go to work every day, the husband doesn't help the wife in the kitchen when they get home in the evenings. She nags him about failing to help her with the dinner dishes, crying, "I can't believe you're so lazy!" Rather than making a simple observation about one aspect of his behavior, she expands it into an indictment of his whole character.

TRYING TO FIX A MATE WITH CRITICISM
AND JUDGING IS LIKE TRYING TO ALTER
A SUIT WITH HAMMER AND NAILS.

Trying to fix a mate with criticism and judging is like trying to alter a suit with hammer and nails.

What About More Serious Flaws?

When I urge you to stop trying to change your mate, I am speaking mainly of minor idiosyncrasies, which, as I said previously, should be taken with grace along with the good points. But I fully realize that some faults are worse than merely annoying or distasteful. Some spousal behavior may threaten your marriage. Maybe she can't stay within the budget and runs up the credit card bill. Maybe he makes major purchases without consulting her. Maybe one has a compulsion or addiction. Problems such as these need to be addressed, and fixing them is imperative.

So how do you get your mate to make the needed change without becoming his or her fixer? Let's look at some ways.

When addressing spousal behaviors that must be changed, it is always more effective to focus the conversation on "we" instead of "you." Make it clear that you are not trying to come down hard or be accusative. Your primary interest is in improving or saving the marriage relationship while increasing your times of connection and deepening your level of intimacy.

Motivating Your Spouse toward a Positive Solution

Usually, the best way to get your mate to change a problem behavior is to make the benefit of the change apparent. By using a little creativity you can assess the problem and find a way to motivate your spouse positively instead of resorting to the negative, ineffective habits of nagging, criticizing, judging, or complaining.

One woman I knew used motivation effectively to achieve a needed change in her husband. He was a nice enough guy, but he followed his father's example in spousal roles. To him it seemed natural that when the meal was over the man was free to watch the news while the woman cleaned up the mess from dinner. His thoughtless behavior aggravated his wife, but she held it in and let it fester. Finally she could no longer stand the personal insult she felt from having to both cook and clean up while he did nothing. So she came up with a creative approach that worked.

Before I tell you what she did, let's look at a few other options she could have tried—all viable, and none that resorted to nagging or criticizing.

1. She could have stopped preparing dinner, instead making reservations at a restaurant seven nights a week so there were no dishes to clean up. When he asked why, she could explain that she is too tired in the evenings to prepare the meals and clean the dishes. She thought eating out would solve the problem.
2. She could have begun serving dinners on cheap paper plates, cups, and plasticware. When her husband asked why they were not using

their own dishes, she could explain that it saves her time and energy that she does not have in the evenings.

3. Rather than go out for dinner she could have picked it up on the way home or had it delivered, using the restaurant's to-go plates and plasticware.

4. She could continue to fix dinner at home but allow the dishes to pile up in the sink. When he finally commented, she could explain that she is finding the double burden of cooking and cleaning up exhausting. Then she could ask him if he would help her with the pile.

5. She could politely ask him to help her clean the kitchen after dinner.

None of these options is bad. Each calls attention to the problem with no criticism involved. But as it happens, this creative woman chose another solution. All she did was to make a simple request with a huge motivating bonus attached to it.

After dinner he sat in his recliner as usual, flipped on the news, and left her standing at the kitchen sink. She walked into the living room and told him that she had been missing him and wanted more intimate time with him. What would he think of watching the news together while they both cleaned up the kitchen? That way they could get to their intimate time in the bedroom as soon as possible.

In your case this solution might not work. You know your spouse, and one of the other options above might be more effective. But in this woman's case the motivation worked very well, and now there is less work for her in the kitchen and more pleasure for both of them in the bedroom.

There is one, staggering truth that may do more than anything to motivate change in a mate: if you can provide that person with unconditional love, if you can look beyond the surface behavior into the wounded heart where the behavior was born and totally accept that person in his or her brokenness, you have a far greater chance of seeing change than if you demand it. It seems that acceptance frees the person to give up some of his or her territory or rights. Your unconditional love and acceptance increases the likelihood that your mate will address the offending behavior and attempt to correct it. Rather than pray for God to change your spouse, pray that God would give you the supernatural ability to be more accepting of your spouse. A heart of acceptance is going to be much more enjoyable for you to possess than one that is critical and judgmental.

Looking at Yourself

Some clients have told me that their solution is to ask God to change the other person. I firmly believe in the power of prayer, and fervent prayer for one's mate is commendable. I recommend that you do it regularly. But as a solution to changing those things you don't like about your mate, it can be a flawed strategy. It can be more a prayer for self than for the mate, because it reveals your inability to accept reality and a resistance to loving unconditionally in spite of imperfections. Furthermore, it often reveals the praying person's resistance to self-assessment and failure to address his or her possible need to be the one who makes changes. The prayer can boil down to saying, "God, make *her* change," or "God make *him* change—not me."

The truth is that neither partner in any marriage is free from defects. If you find yourself disappointed in or disapproving of your mate, whether it's the morning after your wedding night or seven years into the marriage, it's likely that your mate is feeling the same buyer's remorse.

Changes in behavior may be needed to improve or stabilize the marriage. But those changes almost certainly need to happen in both partners. You should not set out to change your mate without looking first in the mirror. No one who marries has the right to stay the same while expecting their partner to change. This means two things are needed: First, you and your mate must let go of your marriage fantasy, as described in chapter 1— and the sooner, the better. Second, both of you should put yourselves in the shoes of the other and realize that the disappointment or disapproval you are feeling is inevitably reciprocated. What faults do you need to address that may be frustrating your mate?

It's important to accept the fact right now that some of the things that bother you about your mate will never change. In fact, most will not change. These irritations or disappointments need not ruin your happiness or your love for each other. But rather than sulk over having to live with those defects, rather than trying to keep your resentment and bitterness at bay, joining a support system such as a Bible study or counseling group will help you find contentment to override your disapproval.

In making this adjustment to our mate's weaknesses, we get help from Scripture. The apostle Paul suffered from some kind of embarrassing or debilitating weakness, which he called his "thorn in the flesh." Three times he prayed for God to remove the affliction, but God did not do it. Instead he told Paul, "My grace is sufficient for you, for my power is made perfect in weakness" (2 Corinthians 12:9 NIV).

> SOMETIMES GOD DOES NOT REMOVE THE BURDEN FROM US. INSTEAD HE DOES FOR US WHAT HE DID FOR PAUL: HE GIVES US THE GRACE AND STRENGTH TO BEAR IT.

Sometimes God does not remove the burden from us. Instead he does for us what he did for Paul: he gives us the grace and strength to bear it. He does this because he knows that exercising patience, forbearance, and acceptance toward our mate makes us stronger, and more Christlike, and deepens our maturity. It also increases our humility to know that our own weaknesses and irritating behaviors must be borne by the other.

Once married couples commit to accept each other's flaws and irritating habits, they discover something unexpected but vital: acceptance does not change your mate. Loving the person in marriage does not necessarily cause him or her to become tidy or punctual or financially responsible or caring and attentive or appropriate in their interactions with others. But acceptance does change *you*, enabling you to love your mate in spite of the flaws.

Be aware of this reality, because you are going to run headlong into it.

If you are not yet married, be aware that once the knot is tied the person you love today is still going to have the same problems you see now, plus a number of other issues you don't yet see. With those realizations, a healthy, strong marriage can be forged that will withstand any flaws or weaknesses in you and your mate.

7

THINGS TO DO IF YOUR SPOUSE
Won't Stop Trying to Change You

- Examine yourself and see if there are habits or behaviors that need some work.

- Change the things that you can and get help for changing the things you can't.

- Evaluate whether attempts to change you in one area could be a result of some unmet needs in another area that you could fulfill.

- Take more time for personal connection with your spouse that will foster more of an attitude of partnership and acceptance.

- Communicate a willingness to grow personally and to grow closer to your spouse.

- Express honestly how you feel when your spouse makes attempts to change you.

- Since attempts to change you may be a diversion from changing self, show mercy and grace for your mate's flaws, minimizing the need to make you look bad so your spouse can feel better about him or herself.

[STOP SEETHING]
IN ANGER AND RESENTMENT

To watch a short video on this subject, go to
7MinuteMarriageSolution.com/5

Just about everyone I know loves the digitally animated movie *Toy Story* and its sequels. In these movies, children's toys come alive and interact with each other when their owners are not there to play with them.

You may assume the credit for this idea should go to some creative genius in the Pixar organization. However, the idea of toys coming to life after hours is older than your grandmother's hat. In the late nineteenth century, Eugene Field wrote "The Duel," a poem for children about two stuffed animals, a gingham dog and a calico cat. At night these toys came alive. The stuffed dog and cat did not get along, and as the night began they were extremely angry at each other. They began to fight, and the poem describes the battle as something frightful, with tatters of cloth and stuffing flying all over the place. But when morning came no trace of either animal could be found. Field ends the poem by explaining the mystery:

> But the truth about the cat and pup
> Is this: they ate each other up!

The poem may be fanciful, but its central idea is not. Anger can eat people up. In a marriage it can consume both partners and destroy the marriage, even one that has lasted several years.

Everyone experiences anger. Even Jesus was angry when he drove out the money changers preying on worshippers in the Jerusalem temple (John 2:13–17). So it's obvious that anger itself is not wrong. Perhaps a better way of saying it is that not all kinds of anger are wrong. Anger directed at a just and unselfish cause or to prevent evil and defend others—which is what Jesus was doing—is not wrong. When you are the victim of evil and abuse, the anger you feel toward this evil is, of itself, justified. But what you do with that anger may be another story. There are right ways and wrong ways to deal with anger. As the apostle Paul said, "In your anger do not sin" (Ephesians 4:26 NIV).

By far most of the anger we see today is not benign. It is toxic and does significant harm. This is especially true in marriage, because anger drives a wedge into the closest and most intimate relationship on earth, causing damage to our marriages and to our souls.

Most people don't realize that anger also damages our physical health. Anger raises blood pressure, impairs the immune system, and increases the likelihood of arterial and heart problems. It greatly increases the risk of depression, even in the spouse who is not angry. Someone has said that anger is like a snake bite: it's not the bite itself that does the harm; it's the toxins the bite puts into your system. Anger injects toxins into the marriage that can eat away at the relationship until there is nothing left. The marriage partners can eat each other up.

Now I am about to say something that you may not like. I'm going to be blunt here and not pull any punches: most of your anger is self-centered. You get angry because you want the world around you to be ordered in a certain way, and when you can't have it that way, you do what an undisciplined child does: you throw a tantrum, pout, or start planning revenge. It's all about you, your entitlement, and what you want right now. You have built a walled castle around yourself with a sign on the ramparts reading, Don't Tread on Me. *Don't violate my space. Don't mess with my domain.* Anger comes from having your expectations dashed, your standards violated, your wants unmet, or your desires frustrated. Your little castle of self is not to be breached.

I know that's not a pretty picture. It makes the angry person seem child-ish and spoiled. I understand that, because I, too, am guilty of building such a castle. When I look at my anger, I don't like what I see any more than you like what I've written here. But the truth is, we all build those castles, and every one of us experiences anger. No one is immune.

Even ministers who preach against anger get angry. I once attended a conference with a respected pastor and his wife. One evening as the three of us were visiting, the two of them got into an argument. As the argument got louder and more intense, I started to walk away, fearing I would get blistered by the heat. But instead they got up, went into their cabin, and continued their discussion. I couldn't hear their words, but I could certainly hear their anger. After a short while they resolved the issue amicably and came out smiling with their arms around each other.

THERE ARE WAYS TO BE ANGRY AND YET KEEP ANGER FROM CONTROLLING YOUR LIFE AND RUINING YOUR RELATIONSHIPS.

As the experience of this couple shows, there are ways to be angry and yet keep anger from controlling your life and ruining your relationships. In fact, some anger shows that the couple cares enough about their marriage to fight for it.

I used to get angry when I came home to a pile of dishes in the sink. I had an aunt who would let dirty dishes pile up and almost fill her entire kitchen, and it was such an embarrassment. So I brought that bias into the marriage. Well, to make things worse, my wife worked very hard at all sorts of things, but she hated doing the dishes. I did not discover that until a few years into the marriage. Once I found that out, I decided that my anger was kind of silly since I was a grown man fully capable of doing dishes, espe-cially when it meant just rinsing them off and placing them in the dish-washer. What a sacrifice (not!) I had to make for both of us to feel so much better because there were no dishes piling up in the sink. And this small gesture had quite an amazing impact on our relationship in other rooms in the house, especially the bedroom.

Couples who don't care don't bother to resolve their conflicts. Most couples, however, would like to resolve them, but they have not been taught the skills for dealing with anger. They don't understand how it works, how to control it, how to resolve it, or how to keep it from doing damage. So let's explore how anger works and see what can be done about it in a marriage relationship.

The Varied Shapes of Anger

Anger shows itself in several forms and at different levels, ranging from simple irritation to violence and physical abuse. Let's look at some of these individually.

IRRITATION

The lowest form of anger, which you would think causes the least damage to the relationship, is irritation. Sandra was not a morning person. When she crawled out of bed she didn't want to talk or be touched. She was grumpy, snapped at Ben when he accidentally bumped her slightly, and slammed the door just a little too hard when she finally got into the bathroom after he shaved.

Ben had his own source of irritation. Whenever Sandra bought a prepackaged cabinet or gadget that had to be assembled, he got grumpy and irritable as he tried to read the directions and make the parts fit like the pictures showed. Sandra learned to stay away from Ben until the project was complete.

No one likes the snappishness and back talk of irritation, but most couples roll with the punches and just take it. It's part of acceptance. But the fact that irritation is accepted doesn't mean it shouldn't be dealt with. We need to be aware that this behavior is a form of anger. If Sandra were to ask Ben why he got so mad when he put together a prefabricated item, he would say,

"I'm not mad! I'm just frustrated by these instructions. Whoever wrote this obviously never put one of these things together." Ben has shifted the blame for his actions from himself to some unknown technical writer. But the truth is, his responses are his own fault. How he reacts to circumstance is his responsibility. He is angry because things are not going his way, and he's got the drawbridge pulled up. The difference between "I wish you'd quit hogging the bathroom!" and outright violent abuse is a difference in degree, not one of kind. Both spring from the self-centered attitude of wanting the world to be like you want it to be. Innocuous as it may seem, irritation needs to be addressed.

THE DIFFERENCE BETWEEN "I WISH YOU'D QUIT HOGGING THE BATHROOM!" AND OUTRIGHT VIOLENT ABUSE IS A DIFFERENCE IN DEGREE, NOT ONE OF KIND.

Overcoming irritation may be easier than you think. There's a simple principle called acting better than you feel. Anyone can act as they feel. That's natural. It takes no thought or self-control for Ben to give in to frustration and snap at his wife when the pieces don't fit together. But as Christians we are called to treat each other with love, patience, and kindness. This call is meaningless if you treat the other with love and kindness only when you feel like it. You don't need a biblical command to do that. The fact that we have such a command means there's something you need to do differently from the way that comes naturally. It also means it can be done, and you are called to exercise the necessary self-control to do it.

The apostle Paul lists self-control as one of the fruits of the Spirit: "The Holy Spirit produces this kind of fruit in our lives: love, joy, peace, patience, kindness, goodness, faithfulness, gentleness, and self-control" (Galatians 5:22–23).

There's a strange thing about exercising self-control and acting better than you feel. Do it consistently and you will reach the point where you begin to feel as good as you act. Your outward actions can feed back to your inner self and recondition it, dissolving your habit of irritation to the point where you no longer feel irritated.

PASSIVE AGGRESSION

Another form of anger shows itself in a behavior classified under the psychological term *passive aggression*. Psychiatrist Richard P. Fitzgibbons, director of the Institute for Marital Healing, tells us the passive-aggressive spouse "pretends that he or she is not angry while at the same time acts passively to vent anger in a covert way toward the partner. . . . The most painful way in which passive-aggressive anger is expressed in the marriages is by withholding love and by refusing to give in a supportive manner. . . . They are often reluctant to admit that they are expressing resentment through passive behaviors."[1]

For an obvious example of passive-aggressive anger, take the case of Tim and Heather in the aftermath of a high-decibel argument over whether to replace their aging sofa. Heather had found one on sale, but Tim insisted they couldn't afford it. The argument broke off with both partners entrenched firmly in their positions. Now they were giving each other the silent treatment, not talking except when necessary and then only in cold, snippy bites.

The disconnected silence led to passive-aggressive behavior by Heather. She let bills go unpaid. She didn't clean house. Laundry piled up. She was in bed and asleep before Tim turned in. When Heather went into her passive-aggressive mode, silence was the least of their problems.

The silent treatment is essentially a power struggle. The clammed-up partner is saying, *I am right; I refuse to give in, so there's no use talking about it anymore.* It is also a way of punishing the other by withholding warmth and amiability. The silent treatment glaringly reveals the presence of the egocentric "I," which cannot be crossed without consequences.

Obviously the silent treatment is not good for a marriage, especially if it happens often or lasts for days. It creates barren gaps in the life-giving flow of love that is vital to the relationship.

A similar example of passive aggression is what I call the "Repeated Nothing Syndrome." As Carl came home and sat down with his wife, Jacqui, to eat dinner, he tried to chat in a friendly manner. But she responded only minimally and with a slight edge in her voice. Carl said, "Honey, something is bothering you. What's wrong?"

She replied curtly, "Nothing." But her cold silence continued. Though Carl tried a few more times to uncover the problem, Jacqui kept responding with "Nothing," until she finally said, "If you don't know what's wrong, then there's no use telling you," and huffed off to bed.

Now, Carl may indeed have done something wrong. He may have forgotten their anniversary or her birthday or accidentally backed over the petunias she planted along the driveway. Whatever he did, Jacqui's cold silence is meant to punish him. The problem is that Carl has no idea why he's being punished, so her silent treatment resolves nothing. It merely drives the wedge of anger between them.

IF PASSIVE AGGRESSION HAS BECOME A PROBLEM IN YOUR MARRIAGE, THE BEST WAY TO RESOLVE IT IS TO RECOGNIZE WHAT YOU ARE DOING AND RESORT TO MORE PRODUCTIVE FORMS OF EXPRESSION.

If passive aggression has become a problem in your marriage, the best way to resolve it is to recognize what you are doing and resort to more productive forms of expression.

Often, however, passive-aggressive people do not follow this advice because they live in denial and refuse to recognize their behavior as passive-aggressive. Their anger, rooted in some unexpressed grievance, has become something they find pleasure in fondling. Even trained psychologists have trouble getting some passive-aggressive people to let go of their secretive anger. That is why this form of anger needs to be nipped in the bud before it spreads and becomes too much a part of the person to be rooted out.

RAGE

The third form of anger is rage, and it is the most common and troublesome form in most marriages. Rage consists of an explosion of temper, causing the angry partner (or both partners) to raise his or her voice and shout at the other. These tirades tend to escalate, triggering an angry response on the part of the other that expands into an all-out shouting match. Typically in these battles, neither listens to the other, as both are totally immersed in their own viewpoints. Rage often ends with the partners walking away angry and frustrated. In the worst of cases it leads to physical abuse and harm that requires intervention from the legal system. I will discuss the horrific reality of abuse in chapter 6.

Controlling Your Anger

Many people believe they cannot control their anger. But it's not true: you can. There are effective ways to do it. First, let's look briefly at a flaw in our thinking about anger that is usually revealed by our own experience. I believe you will see that normal people can and do control their anger.

Paula was easily enraged and quick to explode at her husband, Tony. But she dismissed her prickly nature as "just the way I am" and expected Tony to accept it and not be so easily offended. One Sunday after church she sat in their car in the parking lot waiting for Tony. Most of the cars were gone, but Tony was still on the steps talking with one of the deacons. The church across the street was already out, and soon all the restaurants would be filled.

Finally, Tony began ambling toward the car, still chatting with the deacon. By now Paula was seething with anger. *Why can't he think of me once in a while?* When he finally got into the car, Paula unleashed the earthquake of her temper and dressed her husband up one side and down the other. He drove to the restaurant, and when she saw the line of waiting people, she rocked him again with an aftershock. She didn't speak to him the rest of the afternoon.

The next day, an hour before quitting time, Paula's supervisor brought in a stack of file folders to process. "I need these back on my desk tomorrow morning," he said. "I'm on it," replied Paula, cheerily. But inside she was boiling. *He's had these on his desk all week, and now I have to process them overnight! If I didn't want that promotion, I'd take this pile in there and throw it back in his face.*

Suddenly Paula realized that she was controlling her anger. Yes, she was mad as a cornered rattlesnake, but she kept her anger under control and didn't strike. In fact, she always controlled her temper at work where kind words kept the boss happy and blowing up could get her fired. She could see that her angry responses were not inevitable; they were a choice. She controlled her anger when the consequences could hurt her, but not when they didn't.

Then the thought hit her: *I should treat my husband even better than I treat my boss.* She had proved to herself that she could control her anger, and she resolved to apply personal discipline and the power of God's Holy Spirit to the problem. In a much shorter time than she anticipated, she quit blowing up at Tony and grew warm and kind, removing a huge obstacle that had long impaired their oneness.

Paula followed the principle of acting better than you feel. The positive feedback she got from her mate's responses when she exercised self-control began to recondition her mind. The harmony it produced in her marriage dissolved her habit of anger to the point that when things didn't go her way, she no longer felt the magma boiling in her inner volcano.

Resolve Anger by Resolving the Past

In many cases, simply controlling your anger may not be all that's needed. When control fails to work, your anger is often more than merely a selfish and automatic response to things not going your way. You may have deeper issues that need to be resolved.

Many who face anger issues turn to anger management programs. But that is not enough. Anger management deals only with the surface problem and leaves the root causes of your anger untouched. Your goal needs to be the eradication of anger itself, which is usually accomplished by facing and resolving some issue in your past. The root causes of anger can be complex. If you are habitually angry at your spouse, it is very likely that you can trace the root of that anger to someone else. The issue at hand may not even be what you're really angry about.

When Mark arrived home from work, Marilyn came breezing in with a huge smile on her face. "Look at the dress I found on sale today. Do you like it?" She whirled about, allowing the skirt to flare out like an umbrella. A deep scowl darkened Mark's face. "What in the world makes you think you need another dress? You've got more dresses hanging in your closet than Vanna White. Do you think money grows on trees?" He huffed out of the room and hardly spoke to Marilyn the rest of the evening.

Marilyn did not have many dresses. In fact, she seldom bought anything new. Yet Mark exploded all over her every time she bought clothing or spent money on discretionary purchases—the new towels for the bathroom, the shrub and topsoil she bought for the flower bed, and the "unnecessary" pressure cooker she bought for holiday cooking. These tirades came so often that Marilyn began to pull away from him. Finally she told him that she could not go on this way. He had to get over his frequent outbursts of anger, or she was moving out. She didn't want to move out; she loved Mark and wanted to stay married. But she simply could not live like this. She urged him to get counseling for his anger.

Mark followed Marilyn's advice, and with the counselor's help he quickly discovered the source of his anger with Marilyn. It actually had nothing to do with her. When Mark was a little boy, his father had often come home with extravagant purchases—a fishing boat, a new TV, a new car. His mother always hit the ceiling because she paid the family bills and knew the money was not there. She juggled payments and fended off creditors until finally they went bankrupt, losing everything, and his father left. From that time on his family lived in near poverty. Mark never had the clothes or toys or electronic games or money for class trips and the extras his friends had.

It was only a short step to see that Mark's anger with Marilyn every time she made a discretionary purchase stemmed from the fear that she might plunge them into financial ruin as his father had. His anger with his father was a trigger point for his anger with Marilyn.

Resolving his anger with his father required two actions on Mark's part. He had to forgive his father and learn to trust Marilyn. He did both. Mark had not seen his father since the day his father left. He had no idea where his father was. But it really did not matter. Forgiving someone does not require tracking him down and having a conversation that might produce more anger. In fact face-to-face forgiveness is sometimes impossible.

But Mark, with the help of a counselor, wrote his father a letter. In that letter he expressed all the anger and disappointment he had felt as a child. He let everything he could think of spill onto the pages. He sobbed as he wrote, and at the end of the letter he forgave his father.

Mark brought that letter into the next counseling session and read it to the counselor, again with tears. Then they went out to the parking lot and burned the letter. With that act Mark was free; the vat of unresolved emotions had been drained.

From that point on when Marilyn made a discretionary purchase, he remembered the trigger point of his anger, stepped back, and reminded himself that Marilyn was nothing like his father. She had never given him any cause to believe her spending was out of control—in fact, the opposite was true—and it was wrong for him to be angry with her over a problem she didn't have and one he had forgiven his father for having.

Mark's story makes it sound as if the process of resolving anger is always quick and easy. It seldom is. Angry outbursts become a habit, and habits are hard to break. It takes time and effort. Too many couples, eager to put their problems behind them, expect to resolve long-standing issues quickly and without much effort. It seldom happens quickly, but if the person is open to being taught, anger problems can be fixed. And your marriage is worth doing whatever it takes to make it happen.

Conflict Resolution

Often the big problem with anger in marriage is not that anger sometimes appears, but how the couple handles it when it does. One of the weakest links in most relationships is how conflict is addressed and resolved.

Conflict problems come in two sizes: conflict avoidance and conflict escalation. Either can be the cause of the other. Avoiding conflict allows issues to build to a boiling point, which upgrades them to atomic-level explosions when they come to a head. Conflict escalation, on the other hand, can be such a traumatic experience that it leads couples to avoid facing their issues altogether. The resulting cold war creates an atmosphere of tension that reduces intimacy and builds walls. The solution is not to avoid important differences, but to set ground rules for effective communication when conflict arises. It's a simple, three-step process.

THE SOLUTION IS NOT TO AVOID IMPORTANT
DIFFERENCES, BUT TO SET GROUND
RULES FOR EFFECTIVE COMMUNICATION
WHEN CONFLICT ARISES.

STEP 1: LISTEN

The first rule in effective conflict resolution is to listen carefully to everything your mate is saying—both on the surface and beneath it. Failure to listen is one of the most common causes of miscommunication. As one man told his friend, "My wife says I don't listen to her. At least, I think that's what she said."

To see whether you really listen to your mate, do this two-point check on yourself the next time the two of you attempt to resolve a conflict. First, when your mate begins to speak, do you find yourself getting angry and planning your response even before your mate's first sentence is complete? Second, do you find yourself interrupting and refuting before your mate completes all he or she intends to say?

These common tendencies indicate that you are not listening. Your castle is closed, the drawbridge is up, and you are notching your arrows for the counterattack. When both partners do this, they might as well be locked in separate rooms for all the good their discussion is doing. Neither is hearing the other.

Observing sound speaker/listener techniques can do much to resolve conflicts effectively. The first rule is that one person—let's say your spouse—has the floor at a time and holds it *without interruption* as long as needed to say what she feels.

The spouse should limit what she says to the subject at hand, and it's important that she avoid being accusative. She should talk about her own thoughts and feelings concerning the controversy and not attack her husband's point of view or motives. ("Here is why I think we need to buy that new sofa . . .") That means using "I" statements instead of "you" statements. "I" statements unite, while "you" statements are interpreted as attacks and create alienation and distance. ("You never seem to notice how ragged and lumpy those cushions are.") She should avoid name-calling, judgments, criticisms, and all-encompassing assumptions such as "you always" or "you never" statements.

You must remain quiet and listen carefully and respectfully until she finishes. Though you disagree and may be angry yourself, you must not appear bored or show contempt with body language or facial expressions. Disagreement is no excuse for disrespect.

STEP 2: REPEAT YOUR MATE'S POINTS

Before you present your own view of the issue, you must paraphrase what you heard back to your wife to be sure you understood. She listens to your paraphrase without interrupting, and then she either affirms or corrects as needed. To ensure complete understanding, you should limit your paraphrase to a maximum of three sentences at a time before pausing for her affirmation or correction.

STEP 3: REBUTTAL

When your wife agrees that you have understood her correctly, you make your rebuttal to her original statement. As you do this, your positions reverse, and she becomes the listener, making no interruptions until you finish and then paraphrasing your words back to you as you did for her. The two of you continue this process back and forth until you reach some kind of agreement or resolution.[2]

You may think this procedure seems unnatural. Bingo! That's the whole point. You already know what happens when you tackle controversy by doing what comes naturally. Having an ordered procedure tends to defuse the powder keg.

The Antidote to Anger

Just as most anger is rooted in self-centeredness, the antidote to anger is humility. That means having the maturity to understand that your own point of view is not the only one in the universe. We all have to get over the idea that we are always right. That person you married, who is so different from you in so many ways, has a point of view as well. Humility says, "I must not assume my point of view is the correct one until I have put myself in the shoes of the other and seriously considered his or her point of view with an open mind, directed by God and Scripture."

SOME CONFLICT IN MARRIAGE IS
INEVITABLE. BUT IT DOESN'T HAVE TO
BUILD A WALL OR DESTROY INTIMACY.

Some conflict in marriage is inevitable. But it doesn't have to build a wall or destroy intimacy if partners manage the process in a way that prevents volatility and hurt. In any kind of conflict or anger between the two of you, it is important to remember the apostle Paul's admonition, "Do not let the sun go down while you are still angry, and do not give the devil a foothold" (Ephesians 4:26–27 NIV). And especially take to heart Ephesians 4:31–32: "Get rid of all bitterness, rage, anger, harsh words, and slander, as well as all types of evil behavior. Instead, be kind to each other, tenderhearted, forgiving one another, just as God through Christ has forgiven you."

I can't think of a better verse for a couple to memorize together.

7

THINGS TO DO IF YOUR SPOUSE
Won't Stop Seething in Anger and Resentment

- Evaluate your behavior to determine if there is anything you do to provoke anger in your spouse. Work toward changing those behaviors that seem to be the most upsetting to your spouse.

- Evaluate whether or not your spouse is angry over a lot of little things because of some major thing you have done in the past that has not been resolved.

- Schedule some free time on a regular basis where it is just the two of you with no agenda but to enjoy each other, and during those times steer clear of issues that you know result in angry exchanges between the two of you.

- Seek out a marriage seminar or weekend workshop that could provide some insight into the problem and how to minimize anger in the relationship.

- If there is a serious offense that your spouse is still angry about, be sure you have done all you can to make it right, including some form of restitution that would be appreciated by your spouse.

- If your spouse's anger ever results in physical violence or the threat of it, take appropriate steps to protect yourself and your children.

- Be sure you are taking the time to connect around God's truth that always leads toward grace and forgiveness and away from bitterness and anger.

[STOP TOLERATING]
COMPULSIONS AND ADDICTIONS

To watch a short video on this subject, go to
7MinuteMarriageSolution.com/6

Buck had been married to Gena for over ten years. Though he was a skilled construction worker and made a good wage, they lived near the poverty line because he gambled away their money and then continued to gamble up fifty thousand dollars of debt. But like so many others with an addiction, gambling was not his only problem. Buck ran around on Gena, drank heavily, smoked, and used pornography. He said he was a Christian, but clearly he had failed to exercise self-discipline to keep his urges under control. And now his life was out of control, putting their marriage in serious peril.

Gena was miserable, but like many women she felt she had little choice but to put up with his destructive behavior. She was paralyzed by thinking she had no options. Her shame stopped her from reaching out to explore what options she did have. She was listening to *New Life Live* one day and heard us talking about the need to make a bold move to bring hope back into the relationship. We were encouraging another lady to step out of her fear and into the arms of God to do the toughest thing she had ever imagined she could do. Something about listening to that radio show triggered Gena's courage, so she finally broke through her fears and denial and confronted Buck with the evidence that his life was out of control and insisted that he get help.

Now the relationship between Buck and Gena hangs in the balance, as it does in many thousands of American marriages in which serious addictions create a hell-on-earth for families. What happens at this point—the point of confrontation—is what determines whether the marriage will survive or plunge to its death.

Compulsions and addictions take many forms. We are well aware of many of them because they are so widespread and destructive. These include sexual compulsions, child or spousal abuse, pedophilia, alcoholism, drug addictions, pornography, and gambling addictions. Other compulsions are equally destructive but not so commonly recognized, such as hobbies or career absorption.

What these compulsions and addictions have in common is how they can destroy relationships, especially marriage and family, and the extreme difficulty in overcoming them. A person caught in an addiction essentially loses control of himself. The addiction takes over, and the need for a fix grows so strong that to the victim it seems irresistible. According to some psychologists, a true addiction must have a chemical component— drugs and alcohol are obvious examples. The user's internal systems come to depend on regular infusions of the substance in order to maintain the body's chemical equilibrium. Of course, the problem is that while the body becomes dependent on the substance, the substance is also destroying the body and often the mind as well.

Other compulsive behaviors, such as pornography, sexual addiction, and gambling, do not have an obvious chemical component because no external physical substance is being introduced into the body. For this reason, some psychologists do not label these behaviors as true addictions, calling them compulsive behaviors instead. These behaviors, however, function exactly like addictions. The activity triggers a pleasurable mental or emotional high and a corresponding desire to repeat the behavior. And no matter the original source, the mood alteration is a chemical reaction in the brain.

The problem with chemical addictions and compulsions is that in time, the body becomes acclimatized to the substance or activity and demands higher levels in order to achieve the same high. Thus the addiction problem accelerates, requiring ever-increasing substance or stimulation to produce ever-decreasing pleasure.

In this chapter I will show how addictions and compulsions destroy relationships. Then I will give you direction for dealing with them when they arise in your marriage.

The Destructive Nature of Addictions

I have already said quite a bit about accepting and tolerating each other's flaws and faults. But addictions and compulsions are exceptions. You must not accept just any behavior or condition your addicted mate chooses to impose. Some situations should never be tolerated, even to keep the marriage together. Among these situations are any kind of abuse, chronic alcoholism or drug use, unfaithfulness, and compulsions such as pornography, sexual addiction, or gambling. To tolerate these conditions is not acceptance; it is codependence or enabling.

SOME SITUATIONS SHOULD NEVER BE TOLERATED,
EVEN TO KEEP THE MARRIAGE TOGETHER.

Every rational person understands how chemical addictions such as drugs and alcohol destroy the body, the mind, the spirit, and relationships. Other compulsive behaviors, such as gambling, sexual addictions, and pornography are more controversial. Many think porn or lust, for example, is a private thing that hurts no one. But since coauthoring *Every Man's Battle* with Fred Stoker,[1] I have come to see more vividly than ever how to determine whether pornography is just a private thing that hurts no one. Just ask your spouse. Let your spouse in on your secret of habitual pornography and see if she is hurt. In almost all cases, she is extremely hurt. Most of the time it is as painful as if there had been a physical affair with a person. The destruction is devastating and cannot be denied.

Contrary to the popular image of the typical porn user, pornography is not just a man's problem. According to Marriage Missions International's Cindy Wright, women today tend to hide what she calls their "dirty little secret." She says that "Thirty-four percent of *Today's Christian Woman's* online newsletter [readers] admitted to intentionally going to a website that was pornographic."[2] Note that these are Christian women! This indulging includes both visual images of unclad men and the highly popular genre of erotic novels. Porn for women leads them in the same direction as porn for men—into a fantasized sexual experience isolated from reality and often accompanied by masturbation.

Bob and Lisa were both Christians. When they married, disaster was lurking in their relationship in the form of Bob's sexual addiction. He would never have called it an addiction; he thought his craving for sex would take care of itself once he was married and had a regular sexual outlet. But when he married Lisa, eating the wedding cake did not produce a magical transformation. The problem persisted. He had fallen for the old bifurcation myth that a person can lust and use women or porn for sexual gratification before marriage, and then once married all of those urges and desires will simply evaporate. As Bob learned, it does not happen that way.

On their honeymoon in southern France, of all places, Bob and Lisa went to a beach where many of the women were topless. When Bob booked the trip, he had convinced himself that being on that beach with his wife, the nudity would not tempt him. But you have to wonder about his reasons for choosing that particular place. On their first day he was able to keep his eyes off the women and focus on his bride. But by day two he was leering, lusting, and returning to the hotel room for repeated moments of self-gratification.

For the rest of the week Bob did better. Throughout the honeymoon and for a while afterward his lust eased somewhat. It was more contained, and he considered this to be progress. Sure, he still ogled. He still sneaked peeks at porn, but not as often as before. He congratulated himself that he was now much better than he used to be and much better than other men he knew. Surely God was pleased with him.

Bob's better behavior didn't last. His sexual addiction had merely retreated while his marriage to Lisa was fresh. But with the new wearing off and the ugly foot beginning to appear, Bob began to miss the excitement of new sexual encounters. This led to more overt lusting, more time viewing porn, and finally to his getting caught in liaisons with other women and divorce from Lisa.

Let's explore Bob's standard of moral conduct and see how it led to his downfall. It's one that is common among Christians today. It could be called the "better than" standard of morality, and I regret to say that it is largely the standard by which God's people now live. The "better than" standard is based on what others do or on what I used to do. If I am doing better than others, then I must be doing pretty well. If I am doing better than I used to do, then I must be close enough to God's requirement for sexual morality, sexual integrity, and sexual purity that he feels pretty good about me.

But this is not how God sees it. We completely miss the mark of what God wants for us as long as we measure our behavior by the world's standard of "better than." It is nowhere close to God's standard. He requires a standard that far exceeds the "better than" values of the world.

The apostle Paul clarifies God's absolute standard in Ephesians 5:3: "But among you there must not be even a hint of sexual immorality, or of any kind of impurity, or of greed, because these are improper for God's holy people" (NIV). Not even a hint. That means none, nada, nothing, no trace. And it certainly means "better than" won't cut it. When a man looks at another woman with lustful eyes, the hint of sexual immorality is present. When a woman ogles a man, admiring his face and form and comparing him to her husband, the hint of sexual immorality is present. The hint comes from the heart and blocks the possibility for true and deep intimacy, including sexual intimacy and a solid bond of oneness.

The same principle is true for other addictions. The compulsive gambler must not excuse himself, saying, "At least I don't gamble as much as others I know." Or even, "Yes, I do drugs, but only marijuana. I wouldn't touch the hard drugs like some of those crackheads on skid row." Excuses such as these don't wash for two reasons: First, they do not work. A person who continues his addiction because it's not as bad as others is on a slippery slope. If it's not bad now, it will soon become so unless measures are taken to stop the behavior entirely. The nature of addiction is always to increase, never to remain at an innocuous level.

Second, in God's eyes, there is no comparative standard. His absolute standard is purity and holiness. Addictions and compulsions must be dealt with. They cannot be tolerated. And every one of the situations or rationalizations mentioned above is an indication that a person is moving away from recovery and transformation rather than toward it.

Dealing with the Fear Factor

In spite of the pain and dysfunction that addictions inflict on relationships, some married people choose to tolerate the addiction rather than deal with it. They choose to submit to circumstance and accept their spouse's addiction rather than disrupt their home or jeopardize their security. Their problem is fear, which is in my experience the number-one driving force behind women's acceptance of their husbands' destructive behavior.

Fear was Betty's problem. Her husband was unfaithful, and when she discovered the affair she forgave him without requiring him to get help or counseling. He promised to stop the relationship, and that was good enough for her. She did not follow President Reagan's sound rule of "trust but verify." Later she admitted that she had forgiven him so quickly out of fear that he would leave her. But he did not end the relationship; he just hid it better.

Six years later with no warning, Betty's husband filed for divorce and left her for the other woman. To add insult to injury, he sued for custody of their two teenage children. Betty was devastated, but she mustered up the courage to find an attorney to protect her rights.

Fourteen months later, on the week before the final divorce hearing, Betty started giving signals to her attorney that she was uneasy about continuing the process. On the day before the hearing she told her lawyer she wanted to give up and just let her husband have everything he wanted. Of course, her impulsive and irrational decision was driven by fear. She did not want to go into that courtroom. It was unfamiliar and intimidating, and *he* would be there. She just wanted it all to be over so she could climb back into her cocoon of false security.

In the meantime, she did muster up enough courage to call our *New Life Live* radio show. We helped her see what was driving her decision and how unfortunate giving up would be, not only for her own future but for her children's as well. We encouraged her to act in the best interests of her family in spite of her feelings, and then we would help her with her fear problem after the dust had settled. She took our advice and instructed her attorney to fight for what was rightfully hers. By overcoming her fear, she got an excellent settlement and retained custody of her kids.

Some women tolerate addictions because they fear for their financial security. One woman called *New Life Live* and explained why she had to submit to her husband's serial adultery. "I'm miserable putting up with this," she said, "but I can't confront my husband about it because I have no options. I can't risk a breakup because I have no place to go and no way to support myself. So I'm stuck living with an unfaithful spouse." Like Betty, her problem was fear. But unlike Betty, she refused to face her fear and overcome it. She thought she had no choice but to accept her husband's destructive behavior.

Even in situations like this, women do have choices, as another caller effectively demonstrated. Her husband was an alcoholic who refused to do anything about his drinking. "It's the way I was before we married," he told her, "and I don't see any need to change." She found this answer unacceptable, so she took decisive steps. She went back to school and, though it took three years, got her graduate degree in counseling so she could support herself. When her husband realized what she was doing and why, he took the necessary steps to turn his life around. Sometimes all it takes is for the addicted spouse to realize the consequences of his or her behavior.

Women trapped in untenable situations have other options as well. If she can't go back to school or if children are involved, she can go online or to the local library and look up legal aid sources in the city or county. She can find agencies that provide monetary support during separation from her husband. She can check into women's shelters, some of which also provide legal aid. She can locate and attend an Al-Anon group for codependency. She can develop church-related friendships to find people who can help her with other options. Taking steps toward such radical changes may seem daunting, but it is far better than remaining submissive to the situation and enabling the destructive behavior to continue until it destroys both your spouse and yourself.

Dealing with the Addiction

It might seem that bending over backward to keep peace in a home with an addicted spouse would be a positive action instead of a negative one. But this is not the case. The attempt to keep peace can actually be a home wrecker because sometimes it's necessary to disturb the peace in order to achieve peace. Jesus did not say, "Blessed are the peace*keepers*." He said, "Blessed are the peace*makers*" (Matthew 5:9 NIV). If there is no peace in the home, you must make peace before you can keep it.

Some marriage partners become enablers because they think their addiction-impaired mate really needs their help and support to live day-to-day with the effects of the addiction. They cannot stand the thought of hurting their spouse. But this desire not to hurt the other, though it springs from a good heart, is misdirected. The spouse is enabling the evil to continue— and in nearly every case, to worsen. Though it sounds like an oxymoron, not all hurt is harmful. Surgery to remove a cancer causes pain, but it's a lifesaver. Inflicting pain on a spouse in order to address a harmful behavior can be a lifesaver for the marriage.

People with addicted mates should muster up the courage to make a bold move and disturb the peace by refusing to accept their mate's destructive behavior. Some who have tried everything else go as far as to tell them, "Either you get professional help for this problem or I'm going to leave you." This last-resort ultimatum is not intended to result in divorce (though sometimes it must), but to help the other see the reality of the situation and its consequences and to motivate him or her to change.

If you are married to a mate with destructive or addictive behavior, it is vital to the marriage that you do not allow the behavior to continue. You must confront your spouse. No matter how much you hate the idea of inflicting pain on someone you love, you must issue an ultimatum: "Either you take positive and visible steps to change, or there will be consequences. I love you and I want to remain married to you. But what you are doing now is unacceptable, and I cannot allow it to continue."

This kind of ultimatum sounds harsh, but it's really the path of love. As C. S. Lewis noted, we sometimes make the mistake of equating love with kindness. "Love is something more stern and splendid than mere kindness," Lewis says. "Kindness, merely as such, cares not whether its object becomes good or bad, provided only that it escapes suffering."[3] Lewis goes on to explain that love demands transformation into what God created us to be. Sometimes love must be tough and pain must be inflicted in order to bring about healing. It can work. This kind of tough love can be the bandage that staunches the bleeding in a wounded marriage, rebinding it for complete healing.

When you confront your mate, you can generally expect one of three responses. The first one is, "Well, this is just the way I am. You married me for who I am; now your job is to live with it." This response will likely include excuses for the behavior. "I get pleasure out of looking at these pictures. I can't see how it's hurting you." "I like the way I feel when I'm drunk. I'm happier; it calms me down; I have more fun." Or even, "I've tried to stop, but I just can't. So I have no choice but to go on like I am."

There is a second likely response of him projecting the problem onto you. You might hear things like, "I wouldn't have to obtain sexual gratification outside our bedroom if you'd be more willing to meet my needs." Or, "I wouldn't have to drink so much if you would quit nagging. When you change, I won't need to drink. Anyone living with you would have to drink just to survive. Quit focusing on my drinking and get your own act together."

The third likely response is remorse and promises. He may be truly sorry you caught him looking at porn. He will probably be genuinely remorseful and ashamed, and he may vow to stop. She may truly be remorseful about her drinking problem and promise never to do it again. And those promises may be sincere. But don't believe them. Addicted persons can almost never follow through on such a promise and will revert to their former behavior. The person who has already gone over the edge into addiction cannot be trusted to correct his or her own behavior. As someone has said, "Don't expect functional behavior from a dysfunctional person."

THE ONLY RELIABLE WAY TO ADDRESS AN ADDICTION IS THROUGH OUTSIDE PROFESSIONAL HELP.

The only reliable way to address an addiction is through outside professional help. I have heard of a few people—very, very few—who were able to stop dysfunctional behavior, including addictions and compulsions, on their own without outside help. But believe me, such cases are as rare as white crows. Most people who stop their own addictions are like Mark Twain, who bragged that for him, quitting smoking was easy. He'd done it a thousand times.

The trick is getting your spouse to agree to professional help and follow through. Elsewhere in this book I warn mates not to resort to criticism when trying to get a spouse to change behavior. It almost never works, and it usually creates resistance or passive-aggressive behavior. Lecturing has the same results. Both criticism and lecturing produce a you-against-me attitude with the added disadvantage of putting the two mates in a superior/inferior position.

There are better and much more effective ways to bring about change. In an intimate relationship, you can talk to each other and discuss your problems without resorting to criticism or lectures. Let's assume you're a wife with a husband who is an alcoholic. To bear down on his behavior with criticism will likely drive him deeper into his problem. You could threaten to leave him, but if you have strung along with his drinking over a period of time, then leaving him is not the answer—at least not immediately. Leaving would be unfair because it's probable that you have inadvertently trained him to continue in the behavior you are now rejecting. The better way is to approach him without criticism by saying something like this: "I really miss the way we used to be. I would love to have those days back, and I believe if we work at it together we can get them back. Why don't we start by talking with a counselor or a pastor?"

With this kind of response you are not rejecting your husband or saying he is evil or worthless. Instead you are asserting that you value him and your relationship with him. You are saying that relationship has deteriorated, and you want the two of you to work together toward fixing it. That is accepting the person without accepting the behavior.

This approach says, "We're in this marriage together, so together let's work through the problem and get things back the way they should be." You can find a counselor and attend appointments together. You can find a support group for the addiction and attend meetings together. If the addicted mate refuses, then the victimized spouse can locate an Al-Anon chapter and attend without the partner until he or she learns enough about the addiction to proceed to the next step.

If the addicted mate does not agree to any change and insists on persisting in the destructive behavior, your only option may be to ask your spouse to leave for a time of separation. If your spouse will not leave, state that you will leave unless he or she takes effective steps to treat the problem. Before you make this threat, be sure you are willing to follow up on it. Make sure you have secured a place where you and your children will be safe. Never make a threat you don't intend to keep. And never make a threat without considering all the aspects, including your children, if you have to follow through. You hope the prospect of your leaving will wake the other up and turn him or her around. But if not, you must make good on your decision. Leave and see whether your absence provides enough consequences to force a change.

Rebinding Broken Trust in a Marriage

What can couples do to rebuild their marriage when trust has been destroyed? When he discovers she is having an affair? When she discovers his secret addiction to pornography? When gambling destroys the home's financial stability or alcoholism destroys the family?

If you are the person who has broken the trust, you can expect your mate to stop listening to anything you say or promise. That is what a victimized husband or wife should do, and I hope, for your sake, that your mate does it. You have already deceived your mate, so why should anything you say be credible now?

From this point forward, it's only what you *do* that counts, not what you say. You can repeat the words, "I will never do that again" as often as you like. It means nothing. You can promise all kinds of reform and change: "I'm going to attend Sex Addicts Anonymous today, set up weekly meetings with a professional counselor tomorrow, and join a Bible study on Sunday." Those are the right words; they sound wonderful. But until your mate actually sees you taking these positive steps, your words mean nothing. Remember, you have broken trust, and you no longer have any credibility. You have no right to expect your mate to believe anything you say.

It's only when your mate sees you actually doing these things you've promised over a sustained period of time that your word will begin to mean something. If you live up to your promises for six months, your mate should begin to risk trusting you again. Only a sliver of a percentage of people who last six months revert to their former, destructive behavior, because new pathways have formed in the brain. New ways of dealing with stress and conflict have been developed. And new habits can be secured in a six-month period. If you last that long, your success will show your spouse that you are serious about rebuilding trust and saving your marriage.

Addictions in Perspective

Your mate may sin grievously, inflicting on you deep hurt and almost unbearable pain. But usually that hurtful behavior comes from only one part of the person. In dealing with addictions, it's important to remember that the dysfunctional behavior is only one part of the person's total being. Ninety-five percent of him may be exemplary, with truly outstanding qualities. The simultaneous existence of sin and good qualities within the same person is not a sign of hypocrisy or total ruin. Remember that terrible, wonderful passage in Romans 7 where one of the finest Christians who ever lived spoke of the despair he experienced when wrestling with the persistent sin principle that plagued him. To paraphrase the apostle Paul's agony, he said, "No matter what I want to do, I have this impulse inside me that prods me continually to do what I hate."

Or remember the great king, warrior, musician, and poet David. This man committed the worst kinds of breaches of trust and the most horrendous crimes—adultery, deception, lying, and murder. You can't do much worse than that. Yet David was described as being a man after God's own heart (Acts 13:27).

Then there's the great apostle Peter, Christ's right-hand man who at the moment when Christ faced the first stages of his greatest ordeal, publicly denied his beloved Master three times. Yet Peter became the strong pillar of the early church.

God did not accept these flaws. He dealt with them in order to root them out. King David's family fell apart as a result of his sin, as he coped with rape, murder, and rebellion among his own children. Jesus had Peter make three affirmations of his love and commitment to counter his three previous denials (John 21:15–19). These dark moments in the lives of the apostle Peter and King David did not define who they were. Their flaws and struggles were only a part of the whole person.

The same is true with you or with your mate. If one of you has committed a sin that has breached the trust of the other, it's only one part of who you are or who your mate is—only one part of your relationship with God. That is why it's incumbent on all of us to see the other person through God's eyes. That means when your mate sins, even grievously, you say to yourself, "There but for the grace of God go I." Yes, it means taking firm steps of repentance and reform under the power of God's Spirit. It also means forgiving as you want to be forgiven.

I will close by once again focusing on Proverbs 10:10 as a stark reminder that in the face of addiction, action and not a wink is what is called for to produce a lasting peace in the relationship: "People who wink at wrong cause trouble, but a bold reproof promotes peace."

7
THINGS TO DO IF YOUR SPOUSE
Is Tolerating Your Compulsion or Addiction

- Ask yourself this question: "Haven't I had my share of [this compulsion or addiction]?"

- Ask yourself why you believe you are entitled to continue in this even though it is damaging the closeness you have with your spouse.

- Ask yourself if this would be part of your day if you awoke to Jesus at the foot of your bed wanting to spend the day with you.

- Ask yourself if you are living in survival mode rather than thriving.

- Ask yourself why you have not taken care of the problem if you are so convinced you don't need help.

- Study this passage: "The poor, deluded fool feeds on ashes. He trusts something that can't help him at all. Yet he cannot bring himself to ask, 'Is this idol that I'm holding in my hand a lie?'" (Isaiah 44:20).

- If you are a Christian and you know that self-control is a fruit of the Spirit, ask yourself if addiction could be the reason you don't have self-control in this area.

[STOP FOCUSING]
ONLY ON YOUR INTERESTS

To watch a short video on this subject, go to
7MinuteMarriageSolution.com/7

When I am alone, I am just about the most wonderful human being on the face of the earth. I really have it all together. I find myself exceptionally easy to get along with. In fact, I get along with me better than just about anyone I know. I make no undue demands on myself, and I find myself in full agreement with everything I think (at least, almost everything). I treat myself very well; thus, I enjoy my own company immensely. In short, when I am by myself, I am one incredible human being.

But put me in a relationship with another person and all that changes. I find myself in disagreement or even outright conflict over opinions and demands. I get irritated, frustrated, impatient. I resent the expectations put upon me, and I resent it when what others say and do doesn't please me.

You may think that relationships cause most of your personal problems and create most of your unhappiness. But the truth is, it's not relationships; it's your own self-centeredness just as it is my own self-centeredness. Relationships simply bring to the surface the truth about who you are, because relationships mean you can't always have things just the way you want them. You must either consider the wants of another or plunge into conflict. You have to stop focusing only on your own interests. In a relationship, self-interest must give in to "we-interests."

A primary reason for marriage failure today is that fewer people are willing to give up their self-interest. Without relationship you are in total control. But it's the total control a hollow tree has over its growth. The problem is, a hollow tree doesn't grow, and neither will you unless you are in relationship. Those who close themselves off from relationships tend to develop odd eccentricities, and when you encounter them you sense something hollow at the core of their being. Unless you are submitting your will and desires to another, you won't grow and mature to become the person God wants you to be. It is in relationship that you meet your biggest challenge to dig deeper and scrape out the flaws and weaknesses you've collected as a result of your egoism and self-worship. Relationship, especially the marriage relationship, forces selfishness out of you.

RELATIONSHIP, ESPECIALLY THE MARRIAGE RELATIONSHIP, FORCES SELFISHNESS OUT OF YOU.

In marriage two separate egos enter a bond with the intent that two "I's" will become a "we." But the bond seldom happens smoothly. Since the fall of Adam and Eve, humans have always been naturally self-centered. Though unspoken, the attitude in the heart of each of us is, *I want you to see me as the center of the universe, just as I do.* Each gives little consideration to the other's opinions, needs, and wishes, and both resist compromise.

Let's say you want to spend your vacation at the beach and your spouse wants to spend it in the mountains. Vacation time is precious, so neither of you wants to give up your own preference. Neither can yield ground because it's a matter of control, and to give in is to lose—to lose power and to become the subsidiary partner in the marriage. It's silly to think the two of you couldn't agree to go one place one year and the other place the other year. But easy solutions don't surface when control replaces love.

Sometimes the conflict is not over preferences, but over who is right. Typically it is still over preferences, but those preferences are camouflaged in the language of absolutes. People mired in self-interest tend to see their own opinions as fact. In other words, they tend to be "always right." Thus she refuses to budge on her insistence that they buy a hybrid car because it's right to be green. He insists that the right thing is to buy a gas-powered car because the efficiencies claimed for going green do not work. They could compromise, of course. But compromising couples often end up like the husband who loved whole milk and the wife who loved skim milk; they compromised and bought 2 percent. That way neither lost the argument, but on the other hand, neither was happy with the result.

It's true that compromise can resolve the conflict, and sometimes it works out well. But more often the better way is for one to submit to the other for the greater good. In a mature relationship where love for the other prevails over self-interest, the question becomes not who wins or who is right, but rather *what* is right. What is best for my husband or my wife? For our marriage?

Remember what I and many psychologists and counselors often point out: successful marriage is not a 50/50 proposition; it is 100 percent from both partners. That means it won't work if you are in the habit of thinking, *Why should I be the one to give in? Why must I be the one to do this? Isn't it his turn? Shouldn't she meet me halfway?* If you married to be served rather than to serve, there is not a lot of hope for you possessing a daily sunny disposition. You will be stuck inside the prison of self, which is the loneliest, most isolating prison in the world.

How Self-Interest Produces Conflict

Most conflicts in marriage follow a common pattern of attack-and-defend. It's the natural response of the egocentric self. The castle of self is threatened, so the self-protection instinct kicks in to defend the self and counterattack. Once begun, the process tends to escalate.

According to psychotherapist Elizabeth Dickson, to prevent or defuse these conflicts, "You must be willing to temporarily leave your position (even when it feels unfair, which it usually does), so that you can spend some time exploring your partner's position with them."[1] In other words, get outside your own point of view. Step into the shoes of your mate and see the issue from his or her perspective. It's called *empathy*, and it's a vital component of love. Empathy helps to get you outside your egocentric self and place the other at the center. By exercising empathy you often find that the thing you feel most entitled to is the very thing you need most to surrender. When you are willing to submit your point of view to your mate, it allows him or her to open up and reveal deeper needs that should be considered.

Okay, I can just feel it as I write the words *submit* and *surrender*: some of you women readers are getting wary. When Christian men write about submission, you may think it's sure to bring bad news, putting women in a position not far removed from slavery and indentured servanthood. If you are a man, don't get too excited. This chapter is not going to affirm your male right to trample on a doormat wife. Instead, I think it is going to bring you both together, closer than you ever dreamed.

I also think what I am about to say goes against a lot of teaching on this subject. But I guarantee it is right out of the Bible. I intend to show you how your natural selfishness has got to go if you expect to have a loving and satisfying relationship. And the key is in learning not to do it "my way," as Frank Sinatra crooned, but rather to learn how to submit to each other.

The Antidote to Self-Interest: Mutual Submission

As I get into the subject of submission, I have to make a confession—something I have not shared with a lot of people. (And I have shared a lot of stuff over the years.) This confession may cause you to question my manhood or my taste in sports. But here it is: I love to watch figure skating, especially pairs skating. Think of me whatever you will, but I like to watch two people gliding over the ice in perfect synchronized movement.

Just in case you are not familiar with it, pairs skating may be the most beautiful of all sports. It's an elegant tour de force on ice in which a skilled couple performs a themed program to stirring music.

Pairs skating also displays the inevitable difference in masculine and feminine roles. The male skater demonstrates the strength and leadership of the masculine, and the female models the beauty and responsive power of the feminine. The male is the presenter and the female the one presented. He often holds her high overhead with one hand as they skim across the ice, enabling her to assume various positions that display her grace and beauty in astonishing spins or by conforming her body to the shape of a celestial star. At other times he hurls her through the air, spinning her twenty feet across the ice where she lands as lightly as a feather. Or he anchors himself firmly, takes her hand, and spirals her in wide circles as she floats on one skate with her body hovering horizontally mere inches above the ice like the sweeping hand of a clock.

In these moves the male and female roles are not interchangeable. It would be impossible for the woman to lift the man overhead with one arm, hurl him across the ice, spin him in the air, or anchor him in the horizontal circle. Even if it were possible, it would look silly to have the muscular, angular man presuming to display beauty and the smaller and curvaceous woman attempting to display strength. Pairs skating provides an accurate reflection of realities inherent within the sexes.

Now, here's the thing I want you to notice about pairs skating. When the man lifts the woman high overhead as she assumes various breathtaking positions, who is submitting to whom? Well, you might say, clearly the woman is submitting to the man, allowing him to take control by lifting her, spinning her, and hurling her across the ice. On the other hand, you might as easily say the man is submitting to the woman by assuming the less vivid supporting role and placing her in the spotlight. You can see it either way. Yes, the man is "in control." He's doing the lifting, keeping the pair in balance, and propelling them across the ice. But all eyes are focused on the woman. That's where the central activity occurs that brings beauty and grace to the performance.

Pairs skating illustrates two points that are vital to the content of this chapter. First, just as the man's directing role in pairs skating does not mean he is the center of the performance, neither does the leadership role of the man in marriage mean that he is the center of the relationship. According to Families.com, up until the mid-twentieth century the man was the one who typically supported the home as the primary breadwinner, and it was the woman who was typically the keeper of the home. But now nearly half of homes with children have both parents being breadwinners for the family.[2] Now, in most cases, if both are earning the dough, they both need to take on mutually submissive roles and responsibilities in the home. As they say, "The home is where the heart is." It's the home and family that is the heart and soul of the marriage. And since so often both are involved in supporting the home, both need to be involved in taking care of responsibilities within the home.

The second point I want to draw from pairs skating is that mutual submission is built naturally into the very design of the male and female. Each sex has parts and functions designed to be submitted to the other. The male has the sexual apparatus, musculature, and hormonal influences that dictate his role as the one who begets, provides, and protects. The female has the womb, breasts, and hormonal influences that dictate her role as the one who bears and nurtures. These complementary attributes enable each to submit to the other their special uniqueness in order to achieve a shared harmony.

A prime example is how the woman submits to the activity of the man to conceive a child. Then once conception occurs, their positions reverse as she takes center stage and he submits to her role in the bearing and birthing of the child by supporting her as servant, protector, and provider. Mutual submission works like the steps in an intricate dance between two partners, each with special attributes that dictate differing moves, but all combining to achieve a thing of beauty.

Headship and Submission

By now it may be you men readers who are uneasy. The Bible makes it clear that the husband is given a headship role in marriage (1 Corinthians 11:3). How does this square with the idea of mutual submission between a husband and wife? The apostle Paul addresses this question in Ephesians 5:21: "Submit to one another out of reverence for Christ." How does submission to each other show reverence for Christ? We find the answer in John 13, where Jesus and his apostles prepare to celebrate Passover. John tells us that Jesus, who was God on earth and the acknowledged leader of the group, took a towel and a pan of water and performed the lowly servant's task of washing the dirty feet of his followers. We show reverence for Christ by following his example of submission.

THE PURPOSE OF LEADERSHIP IS TO SERVE
THOSE WHO FOLLOW—TO GUIDE, PROTECT,
AND LEAD THEM TO A BENEFICIAL GOAL.

As Christ's example shows, it is not inconsistent for leaders to be submitters. In fact, that's what leadership is really about. Leadership is performed not for the benefit of the leader's self-interest—to give him power or control or elevated importance. The purpose of leadership is to serve those who follow— to guide, protect, and lead them to a beneficial goal. We elect leaders of our cities, states, and nation to be our servants—to do the essential, unglamorous work of keeping water, sewers, highways, and commerce working smoothly and to provide protection for communities so we can get on with the really important things of life, like establishing homes and raising families.

All too often our elected leaders forget that they are called to be public servants. Instead of submitting to us and attending to our needs, they use the power of their political office for their own self-interests—to enhance their reputations, their pocketbooks, and their ambitions. Power lends itself to that kind of abuse.

Sadly, many husbands do the same thing in their marriages. This tendency to abuse power for the benefit of self distorts the meaning of relationship, headship, and the mutual submission built into our God-given complementary attributes as male and female. No doubt that's why Paul goes to such great lengths in Ephesians 5 to stress the meaning of headship and submission. After urging husbands and wives to practice mutual submission in verse 21, he follows with about sixty words admonishing women to submit to their husbands. (The number of words varies with different Bible translations.) Guys love to stress this passage, and many have used it to browbeat wives into submitting to whatever they choose to impose on her.

For some mysterious reason, however, many men stop after reading Paul's charge to women and ignore the verses that follow. Beginning in verse 25, he continues to define mutual submission with about ninety-five words telling men to love their wives so much they are willing to die for them. Did you get that? Paul uses about sixty words telling women to be submissive to their husbands and about ninety-five telling husbands to love and die for their wives!

Now, if you turn legalist and start looking for the word *submission* in this passage, you won't find it. But think about it: What does a husband do when he dies for his wife? He submits his life to hers. It's the ultimate submission, just as it was the ultimate submission of Christ to die on the cross for us. It's the kind of submission in which you count the value of the other to be so high that it puts things in proper perspective to sacrifice yourself for her. If a woman is married to a man who is willing to die for her, she would be foolish not to submit to him. If a man is married to a woman who submits to him, he would be foolish not to die for her.

Men, if you really want to be the kind of leader who blesses your wife in the best way possible, allow me to offer a suggestion: Short of putting your life on the line, here is the best thing you can do for her—provide her and your family with spiritual leadership and stability. You don't know where to start? Here are five suggestions to get you going:

1. Do what it takes to develop a good knowledge of the Bible. This is a must.
2. As you learn about God, begin to submit yourself to him more and more.
3. Be consistent in your prayer and devotional life. Your consistency will instill your wife's confidence in you and inspire her to follow.

4. Go to church consistently and worship with your wife and family. Your wife will benefit greatly from watching you worship and worshipping with you.

5. Be quick to forgive and seek her forgiveness when you need it. Your honesty and humility will speak volumes to her.

Male spiritual leadership is a primary need in every marriage, every home. The best way a husband can submit to his wife is to serve her diligently by supplying that leadership through his own example. You will bless your wife by leading her. If you do it tenderly, wisely, and by example, she will follow.

Mutual Submission in Action

To explore how mutual submission works in practice, let's start with flexibility in husband/wife roles. As I noted above, it's obvious that some male/female roles are fixed and unalterable: women are not going to beget children and men are not going to bear them. But not all roles in marriage involve our male/female differences. Pairs skating involves many moves that don't depend on the differing attributes unique to each sex. At times both partners skate in parallel, each making the same moves as the other. In a similar way, men and women are called to give up their self-interest and submit to each other in ways that don't involve their differing attributes.

Harmonious marriage requires self-interest to be subjected or at least balanced with the happiness and well-being of the other. Typically, for example, neither the husband nor the wife really wants to go to the other's high school class reunion. He doesn't know her school friends, and she doesn't know his. But because they love each other and each desires happiness for the other, she attends his reunion and he attends hers. Self-interest yields to mutual submission.

Maybe he doesn't like the color of the carpet she wants in the den. He could (erroneously) invoke the headship clause and reject her choice. But instead he lays aside his preference and accepts carpet color as more in her domain than his. Maybe she hates the moose head he wants on the wall of his study. But she swallows hard and submits amicably to his choice. After all, he's the one who has to work with the monstrosity hanging over his head.

WHAT LITTLE THINGS CAN YOU DO TO IMPROVE YOUR MATE'S LIFE OR TO MAKE YOUR MATE'S DAY BETTER?

To enhance your relationship even further, take this principle beyond just solving self-interest problems. You can solidify the bond between the two of you by devoting part of your time and attention to simple things that increase your mate's general well-being and happiness. What little things can you do to improve your mate's life or to make your mate's day better? What comforts or attentions does your spouse value that you could supply?

I remember going to a speaking event and opening up my notes—and there was a little note from my wife telling me she loved me. When I got to the hotel that night I opened up my overnight bag and there was another note. In the morning when I went to grab a fresh pair of underwear, I found another note telling me she loves me. Those little actions go a long way toward melting this man's heart.

If you are a man, it really is the little things you do for your wife that add up to move mountains. That little note left on the table in the morning can make her entire day. Sending her off to do whatever she wants to do at night while you take care of things at home can transform her world. Start thinking about the creative ways you can give happiness to the other person. Do what you want to have done to you. It really is all about those little things—acts of thoughtfulness that create positive attitudes in your relationship.

The bottom line is that marriage was never meant to be a one-way relationship as with a boss and servant or a master and slave. That kind of relationship reflects the tyranny of self-interest, and neither the oppressor nor the oppressed can find joy in it. The way of Christ is for the other's interest to be placed above your own.

But won't submitting your self-interest keep you unfulfilled and unhappy? No. Try it and you will find that it's the sure but seldom-trod path to true relational joy.

7

THINGS TO DO IF YOUR SPOUSE
Won't Stop Focusing Only on Self-Interest

- Remember that the goal is peacemaking, not peacekeeping.
- Rather than suggest counseling for your spouse, suggest that you both get it together.
- The more self-centered the wound of your spouse the deeper it is, so try to understand it and connect with it.
- Refuse to put up with self-centeredness that leads to controlling or demeaning behavior and be willing to take action when it occurs.
- Be sure you express your boundaries and follow through in enforcing them.
- One way to enter into a conversation about your unbalanced relationship is to start with: "This is not working for me."
- Rather than nag or complain, express your desire to be close and connected.

PART 2

THINGS TO START

8

[START EMBRACING]
FRIENDSHIP AND FUN

To watch a short video on this subject, go to
7MinuteMarriageSolution.com/8

My wife and I love to dance! We are not the greatest dancers, but we dance. If we are in a shopping mall and the music is perfect for a swing and a twirl, then we take a break and dance. We have been known to dance our way to the top in a tight elevator while people sigh and laugh and say they wish they had someone to dance with. If the music that catches our ear is slow, we will dance slow. But we love faster tunes where we can twirl and spin under each other's arms. I fold her into me and then I spin her out. I lead, she follows, and for a few short moments the tough realities we face go away. We are each other's, and it is evident we enjoy being a couple.

When our kids are with us, I think they get a little embarrassed at our dancing. But I also think they secretly enjoy seeing the smiles on our faces and on those who stumble upon our romance. Now that our boys are teenagers, they are even getting into the act. We were at an open-air concert the other night and James, our thirteen-year-old, stood up and started dancing with his mom. It is contagious. And it is fun.

Fun in marriage is similar in many ways to romance, which we addressed in part 1. It keeps a marriage from going stale. It keeps couples connected in a positive and relational way. Fun is also similar to romance in that it is not something you merely tack on to your relationship as an extra; it is integral to the health of your marriage. Fun is more than just the icing on the cake; it is a vital ingredient in the cake itself. You need fun and humor in your marriage.

Now, I know that if you are in a stale or bitter state of marriage, the last thing you want to focus on is fun. I understand. It is not going to happen instantly or easily. But just think back to the early days of your relationship. What did you do then that was really fun for both of you? Was it something you have not done in years, like riding go-carts? Was it an event such as a live concert? Was it taking a walk in a favorite park? You must have done a number of things that created fun for the two of you.

A LITTLE HUMOR AND FUN MAY BE YOUR
BEST PATH TO RESTORING OR RENEWING
OR REVITALIZING A RELATIONSHIP.

Imagine what chill might be thawed if you engaged your mate in that fun thing from the past. Think of the message that would send. It would say that you remember and the memory matters to you. It would say that you are willing to try something risky or to look foolish if it might add a new dimension to the relationship or even shake it up a bit. Just the attempt at putting some fun back in your relationship could cause your mate to see you and your marriage in a new light. A little humor and fun may be your best path to restoring or renewing or revitalizing a relationship. It could do wonders for the romance of your marriage.

God Wants Couples to Have Fun

The most important similarity between fun and romance is that both are God-created. And as the following passages show, God deems fun and good humor to be vital ingredients to a full and healthy life.

- "A merry heart makes a cheerful countenance, but by sorrow of the heart the spirit is broken" (Proverbs 15:13 NKJV).

- "All the days of the afflicted are evil, but he who is of a merry heart has a continual feast" (Proverbs 15:15 NKJV).
- "A merry heart does good, like medicine, but a broken spirit dries the bones" (Proverbs 17:22 NKJV).

You think those old crusty Bible characters didn't have a little fun? You think they were all a bunch of uptight Torah thumpers? I am intrigued by an Old Testament passage as it reads in the King James Version: "And it came to pass . . . that Abimelech king of the Philistines looked out at a window, and saw, and, behold, Isaac was *sporting* with Rebekah his wife" (Genesis 26:8; emphasis added). Modern translations flatten out the meaning of the passage by substituting the words "caressing" or "holding" or "embracing" for the King James Version's "sporting." I presume that Isaac and Rebekah were not playing tennis, but somehow those softer and less vivid words in the new translations seem a far cry from that intriguing word, "sporting."

I was a bit mystified by the translators' use of *sporting* until I learned that in the Hebrew, the original word has the same root as Isaac's name, which means "laughter." Therefore, whatever else the word conveys, it must include laughter. In the context of that particular verse, the connotation is obviously sexual, but it goes further and characterizes the mood of the couple: Isaac and Rebekah were playful, laughing, and having a good time with each other.

If it has been a while since you and your spouse have sported with each other, then perhaps it is time to take a lesson from these playful patriarchs. Think back: Didn't many of the things you once did together lead to "sporting"? Did you ever compete in a game with each other and then fall into each other's arms afterward? Did you play pool or Ping-Pong and end up hugging and holding through a good laugh? Did you ride bikes or climb mountains and then find yourself falling exhausted in each other's arms? Whatever it was, give it another chance. Sure, you might look foolish and embarrass yourself a little. But if it gets the two of you out of your self-obsession and into the fun and laughter mode, who cares?

Being a Friend with Your Mate

The idea that couples should have fun, laughter, and a good time with each other brings up an important facet of marriage I have not yet addressed in this book—friendship between husband and wife. Surely you have heard this before, but let's review what friendship means. Friendship is one of four kinds of love that humans experience. Its biblical name is "brotherly love" (*philia* in the Greek). The other three loves are affection (the Greek *storge*), sexual love (*eros*), and sacrificial love (*agape*).

Affection is the warmth and tenderness we feel toward another being. The object of affection can be a family member, a friend, or a pet. Sexual love (*eros*) is to be directed only toward one's wedded mate. Sacrificial love (*agape*) is that deep love that sees the other as more important than the self and is willing to make great sacrifices, including one's life, for the other. This love can be directed toward one's mate, family members, friends, or even toward animals. We learn much about the high value of marriage when we realize that it is the only relationship on earth that embodies all four of these loves.

Now let's hone in on the meaning of friendship, which has much to do with our focus in this chapter. When friendship is present in marriage, it differs from sexual love in that instead of the mates focusing on each other, both focus on a common interest. Lovers look at and are absorbed by each other. Friends look together at some interest other than themselves. Competent sexual lovers say to each other, "What can I give to you to increase your joy and pleasure?" Friends say to each other, "Let's direct our focus toward that object or activity we both enjoy. Let's have fun together."

That object or activity may be a game such as chess or tennis; it can be reading together or walking on the beach; it can be a project, such as planting a flower bed, painting a room, or designing a house; it can be a hobby such as restoring furniture or collecting first editions; or it can be something fun, like dancing, attending concerts, or camping. The point is that lovers focus on each other; friends focus on common things they like and enjoy. Both relationships are part of a vibrant and satisfying marriage.

One reason romance tends to fade is that early in marriage we try to hold on to the intensity of romance without attending to the components that nourish romance. It's like picking flowers: When you cut flowers from their life-giving stalk and gather them into a spectacular bouquet, you achieve a momentary glory. But the flowers soon wither because they are cut off from their source of life. Romance grasped for itself is spectacular while it lasts, but it dies quickly if cut off from the sources that feed it. And one of those sources is friendship. To focus solely on each other to the exclusion of all else eventually wears thin. You must focus together on other sources of joy to keep the romance nourished. No one can long maintain a high level of emotional intensity. Variety in focus enhances the marriage by creating more interests and broadening the range of sources for joy.

This explains why for a lot of couples, the mood right after the wedding ceremony could be described as, "Let the disappointment begin!" It happens all the time. Even the honeymoon may fall flat, especially if you were sexually active before the marriage. In addition, all the tensions that are pent up in the last days of the engagement—things you thrust aside so they won't tarnish the buildup to the big day—tend to come flowing out after the wedding. As time goes on more unmet expectations accumulate. You hone in on each other's weaknesses. You bear down on each other's faults. And if that is all you do, it's no wonder you can end up with so much disconnection early on. That is why friendship, laughter, humor, "sporting," and doing things you enjoy is so important. You can sulk about your sorry situation or you can decide to get active, doing things you both enjoy that may trigger a revitalizing laugh or two.

In some cultures, past and present, husbands and wives don't generally seem to be friends. Marriages in many times and places were and still are arranged by parents, and sometimes the bride and groom don't meet each other until their wedding day. I love the classic musical *Fiddler on the Roof*, but the one thing about it that has always disturbed me a little is that Tevye and Golda, though married twenty-five years and having five daughters together, don't seem to be good friends. They continually bicker and frustrate each other. Finally in the song "Do You Love Me?" they come to realize they love each other, but I never get any hint that their love involves friendship. And that is very sad and very typical of many marriages.

If you have read any of my other books, you are aware that I have opened up about some huge blunders I have made in my life. So I feel that on the rare occasions when I do something right, I have earned the right to tout it a bit. This morning I made a major decision to be a friend to my wife. I was rushing about because I needed to get out the door and on an airplane. But she was looking a little down, as if she needed a friend. I didn't know if her sadness was over the recent loss of her father or something related to the kids. So I went over and hugged her and asked what she needed. She wanted to take a walk with me. So I changed my airport clothes and we went out for a walk.

It wasn't a long walk, but long enough for her to rebuild her feelings of connection and friendship with me and to help her face certain challenges before her. We talked about some tough decisions we needed to make and assured each other we were on the same page and moving in the same direction. I told her she is the best thing I have going and the person I love. We held hands, talked, and returned twenty minutes later a stronger couple just because we took a few minutes to be friends.

FRIENDSHIP FORMS THE FOUNDATION FOR
THE FUN AND HUMOR THAT MAKE MARRIAGE
ENJOYABLE AT TIMES AND ENDURABLE AT OTHERS.

Friendship forms the foundation for the fun and humor that make marriage enjoyable at times and endurable at others. Marriage without friendship may work in some cultures, but not in our culture. If husbands and wives don't nurture their friendship, their marriage can fizzle into a kind of business relationship where daily responsibilities of career and children drain the emotional connection. According to marriage counselor and pastor Bill Hanawalt, "Couples that don't give attention to developing their friendship often come apart. It also creates an opening for marital infidelity."[1]

Everybody needs friends. Having same-sex friends outside of marriage can actually build the friendship you have with your mate. The reason is simple. Friends can help encourage you through tough spots. They can meet some needs—especially those benefiting from the viewpoint of your own sex—that your mate might not meet as effectively. They can help you see things from a different perspective.

Both husband and wife benefit from time spent with friends of their own sex where they can indulge certain interests exclusive to their particular sex. With their buddies men can talk freely about their toys and sports without boring their women to tears. With other women wives can talk of, well, just about everything, especially the things in which even the best of husbands can hardly pretend an interest.

Same-sex friendships can help the marriage not only in this way, but also by broadening the scope of experience each mate brings into the marriage. You can overdo time spent with other friends, but maintaining reasonable connections with them can really help you have a more satisfying marriage. The problems with same-sex friendships emerge when the spouse invests more emotional capital in the outside friendship than in friendship with his or her mate.

Friends Enjoy Things Together

A primary characteristic of friendship is doing together the things you both like to do. When you were dating you discovered you had common interests, and those were the things you did together. This is surely one reason—aside from your irresistible sexual magnetism, of course—that you were attracted to each other. So, the question is, do the two of you still do any of those things you did when you were dating? If not, have you replaced them with fun things more suitable to your age or physical abilities? Or, like so many married couples, have you allowed fun to fade into the background or even disappear in the clutter of cares, responsibilities, humdrum routines, or the so-called realities of life?

I have heard some couples complain that over the years they have grown apart, and they no longer have in common those things that first drew them together. Well, I agree that we all grow and change as we mature. When people marry young, as the majority of couples do, these changes may be dramatic, as both are still discovering themselves and defining who they are. This can mean diverging interests, but it need not mean the couple drifts apart. Even if you develop widely different interests, each of you can make it a point to show interest in the other's pursuits. And you can maintain a firm grip on those things in common that initially drew you together.

I think a lot of couples would enjoy each other if they were more like Alan and Judy. When Alan and Judy married, they had all kinds of things in common. Both loved Broadway musicals, gospel music, historical movies, badminton, and travel. They also had differences. He was a great reader and loved to talk about books, philosophy, and religion. She, on the other hand, loved to spend her time working in the yard (which was drudgery to him). She read little and had no interest in intellectual discussion.

In time Alan wrote more than a dozen books, which were all published, and he was called to speak in various forums and lecture at universities. Judy made an attempt to read his first few books out of sheer loyalty, but she got little out of them. And when their children started arriving, she never got around to reading the rest.

You might think that such a divergence in interests would damage their marriage, or at least cool it considerably. But it did not, because both Alan and Judy focused on their common interests and shared them regularly. They traveled and antiqued together, watched and discussed historical movies, attended gospel music concerts, maintained an active church life and Bible study, focused on raising their children, and kept in close contact with them when they grew up and had children of their own.

Furthermore, they maintained a sense of fun. Sometimes as they moseyed through a shopping mall, Alan would start belting out the song he heard played over the mall's music system, causing Judy to duck her head and veer into the nearest store. If Alan ventured out into the yard when Judy was watering flowers, it most likely meant a water fight.

No one can be alike in every way, but everyone can focus on the important things they have in common and share those activities to the fullest. Though Judy doesn't read Alan's books and Alan barely knows a petunia from a dandelion, they have remained best friends through more than fifty years of marriage. Maybe you have stopped thinking this way and living like this. Maybe you need some new additions to your repertoire of behaviors. Choosing new things to do could spark a fire in your marriage.

Active Fun Increases Intimacy

One of the biggest complaints I hear in marriage is a lack of sexual intimacy. The bottom line is that activity and exertion outside the bedroom often lead to more sexual activity in the bedroom. I have done a couple of book projects with Bill and Pam Farrel. In their book *Red-Hot Monogamy*, they tell us that couples increase intimacy when they engage together in fun activities that involve bodily exertion.[2] Instead of letting your dates get stuck in the rut of going out to eat and to the movies, plan dates that involve physical activity of some kind.

Bodily activity produces endorphins—the "happy chemical." We know that physical activity increases physical health and, according to James White, PhD, "Research suggests that people who get regular aerobic exercise have more sex, better orgasms . . . than non-aerobic exercisers."[3]

Another benefit of engaging in physical activity together is that it increases relational health by strengthening the bond of friendship between married lovers. I don't know whether the better sex is due to the increased bodily health or the increased bond of togetherness—but who cares?

If you have trouble thinking of recreational activities for the two of you to enjoy, Bill and Pam provide an excellent list in their article, "Relational Intimacy" on the Focus on the Family website.[4]

The Power of Fun and Laughter

One of the iconic women's movies of the current generation is *Steel Magnolias.* In this film, M'Lynn Eatenton (Sally Field) loses her daughter to kidney disease. After the funeral she and her small group of women friends are at the cemetery when she breaks down in grief and anger, crying and ranting at the unfairness of her daughter's early death. She says she is so angry she just wants to hit someone.

The friends gape in appalled silence at their dear friend's distress until one of them, Clairee, grabs the sour character Ouiser and thrusts her forward, saying, "Here, hit Ouiser!" The grieving mother stops her tirade in surprise and then bursts into uncontrolled laughter.

You would hardly think it possible to find the funniest moment in a story at the point of its deepest tragedy, but that is the power of humor. Laughter can defuse tension, turn a bad situation into good, or lift a person's spirits when he or she is dragging. According to humorist Arnold Glasow, "Laughter is a medicine with no side effects." And it's a medicine every married couple should take in regular doses.

In one family the young children heard strange noises coming from their living room. They ran in to see their mother in an apron with their father holding her about the waist as he nuzzled her neck, causing her to giggle and squeal as she squirmed to get away. (I believe they were *sporting*!) As the children watched in fascination, their parents lost their balance and fell to the sofa, breaking its frame with a resounding crack. Ruining the sofa was worth the lesson in playful love the children witnessed in their parents. Though they are now grown, those kids still enjoy telling this story.

I urge a little caution here: sometimes couples (especially guys) think that teasing and playing jokes on each other is fun. In some cases perhaps it could be if done with careful sensitivity. But most of the time I have found that such jokes tend to be hurtful and disconnecting. I suspect that partners resort to this kind of humor when they don't know how to connect in more intimate ways. If you are a couple who happens to enjoy playing jokes on each other, the basic rule that should never be violated is to be sure everything you do causes you to laugh *with* and not *at* your mate. The joke or trick must be mutually enjoyable, and never should one mate be the butt of the other's laughter. This also means, of course, that in telling a joke or funny story about your mate in public, you never make him or her the butt of the joke or the object of ridicule. Never!

I believe you should avoid practical jokes completely. Almost all practical jokes are funny only to the one playing them, not to the victim. Never, ever play a cruel joke on your mate (or anyone else). I've seen a few video clips of people reacting to faked winning lottery tickets given as a joke. Those "jokes" do the opposite of what humor should do. They cause high elation and then bring the person down to extreme disappointment. Why would anyone think that is funny? Humor should do the opposite and lift one from negative to positive emotions.

Never play jokes that could result in pain or injury. This includes even the use of fake snakes, rats, or spiders. Some people have irrational phobias of such creatures, and their panic to get away could cause falls or collisions with objects that would result in injury. The principle, again, is to do things where you can laugh *with*, not *at* your mate.

On second thought, I believe we might make one exception to the "laugh with and not at" rule. It occurs sometimes when the other does something inadvertently that is truly funny. What if you're in church and your mate falls asleep, and when his head falls forward he suddenly snorts and jerks upright? Yes, your mate is embarrassed. Yes, according to the humor rule, you shouldn't laugh. But the question is, how can you keep from chuckling? Especially in church where anything funny is ten times funnier.

The answer, I think, is to learn to laugh at yourself. All of us should learn not to take ourselves too seriously and be quick to laugh at our own inevitable foibles. You know that sometimes you inadvertently do things your spouse can't help but see as funny. When that happens, the best way to respond is to join in the fun and laugh at yourself. Where's the fun in taking yourself seriously?

In closing this chapter it's noteworthy to observe that the "sporting" Isaac and Rebekah must have been just the kind of couple that in this chapter I've been urging married people to become. We think of those Old Testament patriarchs as too staid, upright, and dignified to have fun. Not Isaac!

And apparently not Rebekah either. Some women are too reserved or sophisticated to play and have fun. But I see Rebekah as a woman who giggled and ran when she was tickled, but only fast enough to get caught and find great joy in losing the race and the playful wrestling match that likely followed.

As the wise King Solomon might have said, now that all has been heard, here is the conclusion of the whole matter: the couple that plays together stays together.

7
THINGS TO DO IF YOUR SPOUSE
Is Resistant to Having Fun

- The fun stops when bitterness and resentment rules, so make sure nothing you are doing or have done is unresolved between you and your spouse.

- Sit down with your spouse and make a list of five things you both love to do or used to do and agree you are going to schedule them over the next couple of months.

- If finances are a concern, start saving for whatever you can afford even if all you can afford to do initially is rent some old movies you saw together and loved.

- Be willing to sacrifice spending money on something you enjoy so you can spend that money on both of you having some fun.

- If your spouse loves to do certain things that you hate to do, be willing to participate in those things and see if that does not open the door to him doing some things you love to do.

- If your spouse won't do anything fun, you do some fun and interesting things anyway, inviting your spouse to join you, allowing your mate to see that fun things energize you and positively impact the relationship.

- Plan something with another couple and if you have no couples in your life, fix that problem on the way to addressing this one.

$[$ START RESPONDING $]$
ROMANTICALLY TO YOUR MATE

To watch a short video on this subject, go to
7MinuteMarriageSolution.com/9

When my wife and I got married, we wanted to be sure we understood how to have a sexually wonderful marriage. So we enrolled in a workshop conducted by a physician couple, and it made all of the difference in the world. We had waited to have sex until we were married, but once married we did not really know how to make it lasting and great. That workshop really helped us in this area.

SEXUAL SATISFACTION COMES FROM INVESTING IN THE OTHER PERSON'S JOY AND PLEASURE. IT DOES NOT COME FROM SEEKING TO GRATIFY YOURSELF.

There was one concept that blared at us throughout the weekend. Sexual satisfaction comes from investing in the other person's joy and pleasure. It does not come from seeking to gratify yourself. You will naturally want what you want, but the only way you will get what you want is to invest in the other person's needs and desires. I know that is not a new concept, but I stress it yet again because we tend to forget it, and it is foundational in developing and maintaining a rewarding and growing life of romance and sexual intimacy.

Over the course of a few days I watched struggling couples in the workshop start to glow in each other's eyes as their resentments and irritations were replaced with attention and care. And I have no doubt that the glow is still burning in the lives of those who continue to practice what we learned. It certainly is in our marriage.

For most couples the glow of romance starts with a spark of attraction that builds into a raging fire. It is usually an unforgettable moment. How well Clint remembered that moment. He was dating Karen, the woman who was to become his wife, and they were to meet that evening at a sidewalk restaurant in the arts district. Clint arrived a few minutes early, found a table overlooking the lake, and sat down to wait. Minutes later he saw her, and the vision took his breath away. She was walking toward him with her usual grace, every movement the essence of feminine perfection. The rim of her hair blazed like fire from the setting sun behind her. As she drew closer he could see the velvet surface of her face, flawless and glowing. Her blue eyes sparkled like diamonds framed by long, curling lashes. When Karen saw Clint, she smiled. It was good that he was sitting down, he thought, or that smile would have buckled his knees. Surely he was beholding a goddess, a creature of ethereal wonder. Simply gazing on her filled his soul with all the ecstasy he could stand.

Clint's thoughts must have been similar to Adam's when he saw the glorious, newly created woman (and might I add, a beautifully naked woman) God had created just for him. He knew immediately that they were made for each other. He said, "'This is now bone of my bones and flesh of my flesh;' 'she shall be called "woman," for she was taken out of man.' That is why a man leaves his father and mother and is united to his wife, and they become one flesh" (Genesis 2:23–24 NIV). The physical design of the man and woman shows that God created them for intimate relationship with each other.

What are we to make of those exquisite sensations, the glow, the excitement, the awe, the palpitations Clint experienced as Karen approached—

and I'm sure Adam experienced as Eve approached? What are we to make of this mystery we call romance? What are we to make of the euphoria we feel in the intimacy of the sexual embrace? Everyone who experiences these feelings hopes they will last forever.

We're told, however, that the glory of sex and romance will not last. It is an illusion that fades after the honeymoon as the inevitable reality of humdrum routines settles over the marriage like a gray cloud.

But that is wrong! I know it seems to be right: common experience shows that romance tends to fade, as I pointed out in chapter 1. Yet Solomon's magnificent love song gives exquisite evidence that the glory of sexual romance is not an illusion but a solid reality in God's creation. When we call romance a fantasy and the things that destroy it the true reality, we invert the truth. When God created sex, he made romance—that impelling fascination and attraction between the sexes—a reality. Just as Adam and Eve were created to live forever, so was romance. It's true that romance does not tend to last. But this fading occurs not because it's a fantasy but because of the work of our adversary.

In that magical moment when Clint watched Karen approaching, the veil of illusion was lifted. When he saw emanating from her the aura of a goddess, he was seeing her exactly as God created woman to be seen. At that moment Clint's vision penetrated the dulling fog we fallen humans live in and he saw true reality—the glory that God built into every woman and man he ever created. God meant for the relationship between husband and wife to be one of lasting joy and wonder.

There are ways to counter Satan's influence and bring back into our marriages the reality of romance. For romantic and sexual intimacy to remain intact, the love that adores the body must reach deeper to enfold the heart. When inevitable cares and troubles assail the marriage and the infirmities of age encroach, a deeply committed love will preserve the magic. It will enable couples to retain their masculine and feminine glory even when youthful desire and beauty wane. Couples whose souls become knit together never fail to experience the glory of romantic intimacy.

God created in each sex a yearning for the other so strong it's as if the heart of each is a magnet reaching out to draw the other into a mystical oneness. Professor Christopher West eloquently describes the power of this mutual longing by incorporating phrases from the Song of Solomon: "God created males and females with a yearning for love that 'burns like a blazing fire, like a vehement flame' that 'many waters cannot quench' and 'rivers cannot wash away.'"[1] He is describing sex and romance. Genesis 2:23–25 also describes sex and romance. God obviously wants us to find ecstasy in sex and romance!

Sex and romance go hand in hand, and both are highly sensual experiences. The sensuality of romance includes that magical aura, the palpitations we feel at the sight or touch of the other, the fascination of every detail about the form and movements of the other. The sexual embrace provides the highest, most ecstatic physical sensations a person can experience. That is the glory of sex and romance, and that is also its Achilles' heel.

Distrust of the Sensual

One of our problems with romance and sex springs from a heritage of Christian distrust of anything sensual. *Sensual, sensuous,* and *sensuality* have been dirty words for Christians in the not-too-distant past. Previous generations seem to have thought those words should have been spelled *sin*sual, *sin*suous, and *sin*suality. Obviously, equating sin with the sensual is an error. *Sensual* simply means "of the senses." Our whole existence is "of the senses." It depends on the sensual, for there is little we know, feel, or experience that doesn't come to us through one or more of our five senses.

When we think rationally we know that the sensual nature of sex does not make it wrong. God created sex. Yet, in spite of what we know, distrust passed to us from our parents and grandparents often casts subtle shadows over our sexual relationships. No doubt this distrust of the sensual is due partly to how easily the enticement of sensual pleasure can lead us astray. But all good things can be abused; that is the essence of sin. The abuse of a good, however, does not invalidate its inherent goodness.

Another reason we run off the rails with sex and romance is more experiential. Both men and women tend to separate romance from sex, whereas the two are meant to intertwine. To complicate the problem, men tend to separate sex and romance in one way and women in the opposite way. Men tend to emphasize sex and downplay romance; women tend to emphasize romance and downplay sex. I don't mean totally, of course: men enjoy romance and women enjoy sex. But the emphases of men and women tend toward opposite ends of the sex/romance spectrum.

You might think this dual emphasis should work out pretty well. Women need men for romance; men need women for sex; so each has an asset to barter. Men give romance to get sex, and women give sex to get romance. That might all be well and good if you think of the relationship between husband and wife as a commercial transaction. But when it takes that form, each spouse is in the business of getting his or her own needs met, using the spouse as an instrument for that purpose. The emphasis is on the self instead of the other.

A Shift in Focus

We all know that it's better to give than to receive (Acts 20:35). Most people assume that means giving is better for us spiritually because it involves sacrifice. But giving offers an even greater benefit, especially when it comes to sex. In giving pleasure you receive more pleasure. Try to get sexual pleasure and you merely experience a temporary physical sensation, which eventually becomes stale and meaningless by repetition. That is why men and women who sleep around perpetually seek new thrills by moving on to new partners. They hope variety will counter the inevitable dulling of repetitive sensation.

The focus of a loving married couple, on the other hand, is not on receiving tingling sensations but on expressing love for the partner. This means that in the sexual embrace, the ecstasy is multiplied because it comes not solely from physical sensation but from the act of giving pleasure to the other. The pleasure is further amplified by the sense of oneness, the experience of shared being, the interplay of personalities, and giving to and receiving from the other exactly what each sex lacks and needs.

This is how couples who commit solely to each other avoid the staleness of repetition and find in sex a continually growing bond and deepening intimacy that achieves the true joy God meant the sexes to find in each other.

The apostle Paul tells us that "husbands ought to love their wives as their own bodies. He who loves his wife loves himself. After all, no one ever hated their own body, but they feed and care for their body" (Ephesians 5:28–29 NIV). If you love your wife's body as you love your own, you will focus on giving her all the pleasure you can. Forget great sex and focus on her, and you stand a better chance of having great sex. When she forgets romance and focuses on him, she stands a better chance of experiencing real romance.

In another passage, Paul makes this principle of husbands and wives giving to each other explicitly sexual. Notice how the focus is entirely on how both married partners should dedicate themselves to the needs of the other. There is no hint here of using sex to achieve one's own satisfaction. Nada. His body belongs to her, and hers to him. It's all about giving one's self to the other, which is the foundational principle of sex and romance in marriage (1 Corinthians 7:3–5).

Romance 101 for Men

Okay, men, now that we have established the basic principle of mutual giving, let's get down to some really practical stuff. Since women crave romance and men have somehow acquired a reputation for being romantically challenged, let's spend a moment looking at what we can do about that little problem.

Here is the key: we tend to make the same mistake in romance that many people make in religion. We know that for a person who truly loves God, worship is not just a Sunday-only thing; it's a way of life. It means being continually God-conscious and pleasing him in all your relationships, activities, transactions, and recreations.

Your relationship with your wife should work in exactly the same way. Romance is not something you do only on romantic occasions; it must be a way of life. It's the way you conduct yourself in your relationship with your wife. You can't spend all week being a slob, neglecting her, ignoring her needs, spending time away from her, and then on Friday night suddenly turn on the charm and wine her and dine her with the intent of getting her to turn on to you when you turn out the light.

One song in Gershwin's great folk opera *Porgy and Bess* is "A Woman is a Sometime Thing." It's a lyrical way of saying that the moods and desires of a woman change dramatically. Maybe she's a sometime thing sexually because you are a sometime thing romantically. Romance can't be just a sometime thing that you turn on when your libido is revving in high gear. It has got to be woven into the essence of your entire relationship with her.

WHAT REALLY FUELS ROMANCE IN A MARRIAGE IS FOR EACH MATE TO PUT THE OTHER FIRST AND BE CONTINUALLY ATTENTIVE TO THE OTHER'S NEEDS.

Don't worry, I'm not about to recommend sending flowers or a card every day or taking her on dates twice every week. These romantic perks are merely the icing on the cake—not the cake itself. They are good and needed on occasion, but they are not the essence of romance. What really fuels romance in a marriage is for each mate to put the other first and be continually attentive to the other's needs.

This means being your wife's companion and friend, putting her first as the one you really want to be with. It means being her confidante, the one with whom you share your deepest secrets, hopes, and desires, and the one in whom she confides without fear of betrayal or judgment. It means caring for her well-being, watching that she is not overworked and attending to her health. It means being thoughtful, kind, and patient with her. It means helping when she needs help, caring for her when she's sick, cheering her up when she's down, laughing with her when she's happy, and exulting in her accomplishments. It means observing the common courtesies of opening doors and seating her at tables. I could go on, but I hope you get the idea.

You may not see these attentions as romance, but believe me, she will. Because if you do all these things, they add up to show that you cherish her, that she is important to you. What makes her melt in your arms is not the flowers or the chocolates; it's becoming a man she admires, respects, looks up to, and depends on. This is what builds a solid foundation of true romance.

Now men, please notice: I said these acts of care you perform for your wife are the *foundation* of romance. They make the cake I spoke of above. But don't get the idea that you can ignore the icing—the flowers, chocolates, cards, and candlelight dinners—or whatever it takes to speak the romantic love language of your spouse. It is crucial that you don't forget birthdays, anniversaries, Valentine's Day, or Mother's Day. That's basic. But it enhances romance when you give her flowers, cards, or take her out on occasions that are not special. She expects you to remember the special days, but when you remember her at other times it makes her feel special for who she is, not just because you did your husbandly duty on a holiday.

And by all means, tell your wife how much you love her. Like voting in a Chicago election, you should do it early and do it often. You may assume your wife knows how much you love her, but hearing you say the words is like Godiva chocolates to her soul. I suppose it's remotely possible that you could say it too often, but with most men that's about as likely as getting hit by a falling meteor.

Yes, I know you're a mighty hunter and a macho honcho, and romancing isn't your cup of tea—uh, I mean mug of grog. To that I have two answers. First, romance is not as unmanly as you think. Masculine clunkyness in romance is something of a modern thing. In the 1700s, 1800s, and early 1900s, educated men in the better parts of society prided themselves on their romantic abilities. It was also part of court life among knights of the Middle Ages. In almost any movie of those periods you will see men dancing, singing in drawing rooms, playing parlor games with women, quoting poetry, writing florid letters, and dressing to the hilt. Even as late as World War I, the most popular reading among British soldiers in the trenches of

France was Jane Austen's novels. Men do have a historical romantic streak in them. It may now be latent, but it's there.

My second answer to your resistance to romance is that you can learn to do it. We males are not so dense that we can't learn new tricks. And if we expect to live successfully with a woman, we've got to learn everything we can about them. We're not living in some remote Amazon jungle tribe where the men smoke their reed pipes in the all-masculine security of their own collective hut. We have chosen to share a house with a female, which means the atmosphere percolates as much with estrogen as testosterone. We must adapt ourselves to breathing it. It won't hurt you to switch from ESPN, pop a bowl of popcorn, and watch a few chick flicks with her.

Becoming One with Your Spouse

Eva loved to go "antiquing," but her husband, Matt, hated it. He couldn't see the point of spending a Saturday traipsing through endless rows of dusty junk in one shop after another, looking for nothing in particular. Eva went by herself a time or two, but soon she quit going at all. Matt felt bad about her giving up something she so enjoyed, because he knew it was simply because she didn't like spending that much weekend time away from him.

So one Saturday morning he got up, brewed the coffee, and brought a cup to the bed. "Get up, Eva," he said, handing her the cup of steaming coffee. "We're going to spend the day antiquing." She survived the shock, got ready, and that day they hit every antique mall in two counties. Eva was excited and bubbly the whole day, often taking his hand or squeezing his arm. When they lunched at one of the mall's froufrou restaurants, he was struck by the soul-melting softness of her gaze across the table. *She really loves this*, he thought. *It was worth it.* And that night after they got home and into bed, he found that it was *definitely* worth it!

Guys, if you make this adaptation to the mysterious world of femininity, I'm pretty sure you will like the result.

Something will always be missing in your marriage if the only time you want to be "one flesh" with your spouse is when you crawl into bed at night.

That will show her you are not truly one with her in every way. You are simply using her as an instrument to achieve sensations in your genitals. If that's all you want from marriage, I feel sorry for you, because you are missing out on one of the greatest gifts that God has given man—the incredible joy of being truly one with a woman in every way. When that oneness includes love and romance—by which I mean all the mental, emotional, and relational connections I noted above—the sexual act becomes not merely a matter of genital friction but an ecstatic oneness that permeates the entire bodies and souls of both persons. You don't want to miss out on this wonderful, God-given gift. The Bible makes it clear that sex is a gift God means for a married couple to enjoy. As Proverbs 5:18–19 says, "Let your fountain be blessed, and rejoice with the wife of your youth. As a loving deer and a graceful doe, let her breasts satisfy you at all times; and always be enraptured with her love" (NKJV).

Your wife won't welcome your penis into her body until your love has entered her heart to prepare the way. That leads to my most famous equation: erection minus connection equals rejection. It's not easy to argue with that, is it? It means building and maintaining that foundation of romance. If, from a sense of duty, she lets you enter her body sexually when you have not entered her heart emotionally, she will see it as a selfish intrusion, and she will build up resentment and resistance to your sexual advances. If she often has a headache, consider the possibility that you are putting your own sexual wants ahead of your care for her. Putting her first may cure those headaches faster than any aspirin. Keep it up and she may start dragging you to the bedroom.

Sex 101 for Women

Women, you have probably already learned that your husband's sexual desire is hair-triggered, ready to fire at the slightest pressure. But a woman's sexual desire is seldom as pressing or obvious. More buttons have to be pushed and more switches flipped to release the firing mechanism. That doesn't mean your desire is less than his—both men and women love sex—but in you it is generally planted deeper, and it must be drawn out. For this reason, most women don't share the strong urgency for sex that men feel, and this is one of the sources of frustration between married couples.

I urge you not to allow this tension to cause you to abandon hope of sexual pleasure. Don't push sex to the side or allow your sexuality to go dormant. Don't fall into the easy habit of letting him have his sex on your disengaged body. That will build up resentment on your part and dissatisfaction on his.

One way to resolve the tension of differing levels of desire is for you to allow him to draw out your sexual desire through foreplay—to bring you up to the point where your desire matches his. You may go to bed thinking you have no desire for sex tonight, when in fact it may be there but too far beneath the surface to be recognized. It's possible that if you allow your husband to draw it out, your desire may soon match his.

It's also possible—in fact, I think it's probable—that he will not at first know how to do this. Many women seem to think men have built-in instincts enabling them to know how to please a woman sexually. Unfortunately, men seem to think it, too, because over the years I have heard so many women complain that their men are sexually confident but utterly incompetent. They think they know how to satisfy a woman, but they end up satisfying only themselves. The complaint I hear most often is, "It's all about him. He doesn't care what I want or what works for me."

That complaint doesn't necessarily mean the husband is being intentionally self-focused; he simply needs to learn something he thinks he knows but doesn't. Men do not automatically know how to satisfy a woman sexually. It's a learned skill. While your husband may learn much before marriage through reading or advice, he cannot know exactly what pleases you personally. Every woman is different in terms of what arouses her and what doesn't. You must be your husband's teacher. Communicate to him your sexual needs. Let him know what works and what doesn't.

Many women feel reticent about talking of such things. If that's your problem, I urge you to overcome it. Think of it as a way of sharing a deep intimacy with your husband. It's something that only you and he know, that only you and he can discuss, that only the two of you can learn by experimentation. It helps to remember that sexual pleasure is God's design. Talking about it with the man he gave you to provide that pleasure is perfectly acceptable, and it can even be enjoyable.

While men tend to be sexually confident even when they have little reason to be, women tend to lack sexual confidence even when they have good reason to possess it. Usually a woman's lack of sexual confidence involves body issues. Because of today's impossible standards for female beauty, few women think their bodies measure up to the air-brushed models they see in the media.

This was Valerie's problem. She was about fifteen pounds over the "ideal" (whatever that means) weight for her height. On her wedding night, she was too embarrassed to let her husband see her naked, so she undressed and slipped under the covers before he came out of the bathroom. But when she gave in to his pleading and reluctantly uncovered, she could tell by the light of excitement in his eyes and the tremor of his voice when he whispered, "Wow!" that the sight of her body was a real feast for him. She never worried about her body again.

It would help women to know that the ideal set by media models is a rarely achieved, virtually impossible standard. It should help even more to realize that few men like this standard as well as people assume. What men like in the female body is all over the board, from heavy to thin, tall to short, hippy to slender, big-breasted to small-breasted. To see the truth of this, take a brief excursion into art history and compare Peter Paul Rubens's painting of Eve[2] to that of Lucas Cranach.[3] The two Eves are as different as marshmallows and toothpicks, yet each was the ideal for the artist's time and place.

You may feel insecure about your body because it is augmented or because it is not, because it does not look anything like Barbie or it looks too much like her. But give yourself a break. What turns on almost every man I know is a wife's willingness. So just relax and accept yourself as you are. If you accept yourself and show confidence in your appearance, he will accept it as well.

Dos and Don'ts for Mutually Satisfying Sexuality

There are not many rules for what a husband and wife should or shouldn't do in the bedroom, but there are a few that should be observed for mutually satisfying sex. Here are some practical suggestions.

Never use sex as a bargaining chip to get something you want from your mate, and never withhold sex as punishment for some offense he or she has committed. This turns sex into a bartering commodity instead of a mutually enjoyable experience that one gives freely to the other.

Never push your mate into sex when it's clearly not wanted. The reason for your spouse's not wanting sex may or may not be valid. It could be physical discomfort, the wrong place, the wrong time, or some mental or emotional distraction involving work or family. It could be some issue between the two of you that first needs to be resolved. When one wants the connection and the other doesn't, sex will not be a mutually enjoyable experience.

IF YOUR PARTNER DOESN'T WANT TO DO
IT, DON'T PUSH. ALWAYS DO ONLY WHAT IS
MUTUALLY SATISFYING AND ENJOYABLE.

Never push your mate into modes of sex that he or she finds repelling or uncomfortable. Variety and experimentation are fine when they don't involve harm, perversion, humiliation, or risk to health. But if your partner doesn't want to do it, don't push. Always do only what is mutually satisfying and enjoyable.

Again I urge women to tell their husbands what works for them and what doesn't. Husbands, if she doesn't tell you, then make it a point to ask. Learn your mate's sexual response triggers. If she cannot overcome her reticence to tell you, then learn what you can about women's sexual responses in books or talk to your pastor or counselor. And this works the other way as well. Wives need to know what turns their husbands on and, for practical reasons, also what slows him down so he won't peak before you are ready.

Let him tell you what works and what doesn't as the two of you experiment and learn through practice.

Finally, don't expect the same experience in every sexual encounter. Intensity waxes and wanes. Moods change, depending on what the day or week has been like. Sometimes sex may be deep, slow, and romantic. At other times it may be frenzied and urgent. At yet other times it may be playful and accompanied by lightheartedness and laughter. The key to satisfying sex is for both of you to learn to expect nothing but to enjoy what is given.

THINGS TO DO IF YOU AND YOUR SPOUSE
Are Not Experiencing Sexual Satisfaction

- Be sure you are working through areas of bitterness and resentment so that unforgiveness is not a barrier to sexual intimacy.

- If forgiveness is not appropriate because you are still being hurt through betrayal or abandonment, ask your spouse to get help and if the problem is extremely bad, demand it.

- Be sure you are tending to each other's needs outside the bedroom. Initiate romance early in the day and maintain that all day long.

- Eliminate interference when you do have times of intimacy together.

- Continue to remind each other of the good things about each other and the relationship.

- Sexual stagnation is often a symptom of a much bigger problem so get help for all of the other issues that manifest themselves in sexual dissatisfaction.

- Be sure that pornography or erotic novels have no place in your marriage.

$\left[\text{START EXPRESSING}\right]$
GRACE AND FORGIVENESS

To watch a short video on this subject, go to
7MinuteMarriageSolution.com/10

Forgiveness within marriage is an act that binds two people together in the midst of their failures and in spite of their imperfections. Without forgiveness, there is no hope for a couple to have a good or godly marriage. Forgiveness can be painful, and sometimes it seems almost impossible. But with God's help it can be accomplished at the right time and in the right way. When forgiveness occurs, the whole relationship is transformed. When it is not there, relational deterioration can be fast and furious and lasting.

I met with a woman who was extremely distraught over how bitter and ugly her marriage had become. She and her husband had been a happy couple. They had met during their freshman year of college, dated all four years, and married after graduation. They went through some early adjustments but seemed to grow closer in the first year. Then there was a stalling out of the relationship. They grew stagnant, less connected, and much less satisfied. She began to poke and prod, asking him about what was different and how she could help. He resisted at first, but his shame finally motivated him to reveal what he had kept from her for quite some time.

He explained that just before they married, on the trip he took to the coast with his buddies for one last single-guy road trip, he had made a horrible mistake. He had a few drinks one afternoon, the same afternoon that a woman approached him on the beach at sunset. Somehow he ended up in her room, and he had sex with her. He said it was the most shameful thing he had ever done and begged his wife to forgive him.

But she could not. They had been faithful all through college and she honored his sexual integrity. Their bond was sacred long before they married and he broke it. She could not get out of her head him seeing and touching someone more beautiful and more captivating than her. It did not matter to his wife that they were not married at the time of her husband's indiscretion. He had betrayed her in the worst way she could imagine, and she could not imagine finding a way to forgive what to her was unforgivable. The tough reality she would have to face was that unless she moved to forgive him and accept him, there was no way things were going to get better.

Failure to forgive creates resentment, resentment hardens into a grudge, and grudges destroy not only relationships, but also the well-being of the grudge-holder.

———

THERE IS NO ONE-SIZE-FITS-ALL WAY TO DEAL WITH SPECIFIC PAST HURTS. THE NATURE OF THE HURT AND ITS EFFECT ON YOUR PRESENT RELATIONSHIP DICTATES HOW IT SHOULD BE HANDLED.

———

There is no one-size-fits-all way to deal with specific past hurts. The nature of the hurt and its effect on your present relationship dictates how it should be handled. But there is one necessary component to healing no matter what kind of hurt you are dealing with, and that is forgiveness. (If you are having trouble forgiving a wound from the past, you might want to reread chapter 2 and follow it with this chapter.)

Nowhere is forgiveness more needed than in marriage. You may be the most perfect husband since Adam or the winner of the wife-of-the-year award, but you can be sure that you have done things and will do things that hurt your mate. It's as certain as dogs chase cats. And that hurt can erect a wall between the two of you that can be torn down only by forgiveness. Failure to forgive reinforces the wall, blocking marital harmony and preventing closeness. Each unresolved conflict or unforgiven hurt adds a brick to the wall and prolongs your emotional separation.

I am convinced that forgiveness benefits the forgiver as much as or more than the forgiven. If you nurse a hurt or hold on to it with resentment, anger, or thoughts of revenge, it's like swallowing acid. It will eat at you until it destroys you from the inside. Bitterness will undermine your happiness, your marriage, and your physical health. When you forgive, you put away all thoughts of retribution or revenge.

As mentioned earlier, the first step in dealing with hurts in a marriage is to develop sensitivity to your mate's hurts and learn to understand your own. This means delving into the cause of the hurt and the impact it has had. This commitment to understanding enables you to separate the problem from the person, which allows you to hate and attack the problem without hating or attacking the person. You learn to see your mate's hurtful actions not as personal attacks, but for what they are—the spill-off from an overflow of pain. This more accurate viewpoint makes it much easier to take the second step, which is to forgive.

Separating the sin from the sinner was what Jesus did for the Samaritan woman at the well in John 4. This woman felt too shamed by her sins to mix with decent women who drew their water at the communal well in the cool of the morning. She slipped out in the heat of the day to avoid their snubs and stares. But Jesus knew the cause of her pain. Before living with her present partner, she'd had five husbands and suffered five heartbreaking rejections. Jesus understood her past, loved her in spite of it, and forgave her.

In this incident Jesus models to us how we should treat all erring people, and that must apply especially to our own mates. As the apostle Paul tells us, "As God's chosen people, holy and dearly loved, clothe yourselves with compassion, kindness, humility, gentleness and patience. Bear with each other and forgive one another if any of you has a grievance against someone. Forgive as the Lord forgave you. And over all these virtues put on love, which binds them all together in perfect unity" (Colossians 3:12–14 NIV).

Are There Limitations to Forgiveness?

What should you do when you forgive your mate for an offense against you, and then he turns right around and does the same thing again? This question has apparently puzzled people since Bible times, because in Matthew 18 we read of the apostle Peter asking Jesus, "Lord, how many times shall I forgive my brother or sister who sins against me? Up to seven times?" Peter obviously thought seven consecutive forgivings would be quite generous. If my wife kept on committing the same offense, forgiving her seven times seems overly generous to me. But it didn't to Jesus. He answered Peter, "I tell you, not seven times, but seventy-seven times" (vv. 21–22 NIV).

Whoa! That's really a test of patience, Lord. I guess that means I've got to bite my tongue, hold my temper, and keep forgiving my wife until that seventy-eighth offense, and then I can finally let the hammer down. Right? Wrong! What Jesus actually meant was that there are no limits on forgiveness. Come to think of it, that's a very good thing. Instead of thinking how irksome it is to have to forgive someone over and over, I need to think about how many times I sin against God. Suddenly I become eternally thankful that he forgives over and over again. What I must not forget is that I should be more than willing to pass on that same forgiveness to others—especially to my mate. In a relationship as close as marriage, forgiveness is a continuing need. Both you and your mate must freely exercise it again and again and again.

The Difference between Forgiving and Allowing

But while there are no limitations to the principle of forgiveness, that does not mean any behavior is to be tolerated. Let's explore the difference between forgiving and allowing.

If a man is married to an alcoholic wife, he may think that forgiving her of this behavior means accepting it and just learning to live with it. That is not the case at all. You forgive her because you realize that you are not her judge. That is, you do not condemn her for her behavior or hold it against her as resentment in your own heart. If you have gone through the process of understanding her, you will even empathize with the pain that led her into drinking. But if you allow the behavior to continue, you are doing great harm to her and to your marriage. To forgive and allow destructive behavior to continue is not the way of love. It's called enabling, or codependence.

If a woman is married to a physically or emotionally abusive husband, the same principle applies. She can forgive the person, but she must not accept the behavior or allow it to continue because it can cause great harm to her and their children. It is imperative that when addictions or abuse are involved, steps must be taken to stop the behavior. This may include treatment and joining a twelve-step program. If these options are refused, there must be consequences to the behavior. In most cases, it's best that the two separate until the problem is thoroughly resolved.

Note that Jesus did not accept the immoral behavior of the Samaritan woman. He addressed it head-on and dealt with it. That is why you should never "forgive and forget." Forgive, yes; but to forget—if such a thing were even possible—would be foolish. Forgetting would set you up to be victimized again. To forget or to act like you forget means there are no consequences to the offending behavior. It signals that the offending spouse is not required to make any change. On the other hand, forgiving and not forgetting motivates the couple to establish new boundaries to prevent recurrence of the offense.

Not forgetting does not mean, however, that when the person is working on resolving the problem that you hold back one iota from complete forgiveness. To be authentic, forgiveness must be total and unreserved. That means, even though you do not forget, you must not in future disagreements throw the offense back into the face of your mate or use it as ammunition. This shows that some residue of resentment remains lodged in your heart. Couples often do this almost unwittingly in arguments by using the terms "you always" and "you never." "You always take your mother's side against me," or "You never do anything I want to do." Terms such as these show that the forgiveness is not complete.

Why Is It So Difficult to Forgive?

Forgiving serious offenses is not easy. If you find that you cannot simply make the decision to forgive and have it happen instantly as if you had waved a magic wand, don't despair or beat yourself up for your spiritual shallowness. Forgiveness is a process that takes time, work, and diligent prayer. But it is worth the effort because you cannot find healing without it.

FORGIVENESS MUST BE ACCOMPLISHED
WITHOUT ACCEPTING OR CONDONING
THE HURTFUL BEHAVIOR.

You may be reluctant to forgive because forgiveness seems too much like an undeserved favor you grant to the offending mate. It seems that you are letting him or her off the hook, as if the offense was of no consequence. That is not the case at all. Forgiveness must be accomplished without accepting or condoning the hurtful behavior. Forgiving without setting boundaries for future behavior and requiring change—and even in appropriate cases, reparation—is a sure setup for repetition of the hurt.

Another reason we are reluctant to forgive is that we find a certain kind of self-justification in holding on to blame. As long as I can blame the other person for what he or she did to me, then I am off the hook. I bear no responsibility for what happened to cause my resentment. I can evade my own sense of guilt by putting it all on that other person who wronged me.

At New Life Ministries, we conduct Women in the Battle weekend workshops for women who have been betrayed by their husbands' lack of sexual integrity. Many of these women were just living their lives and happily doing their duty in blissful ignorance until they discovered that their husbands lived in another sexual world they were not aware of. These women are understandably devastated by the horrific revelations that come to the surface. Their anger and grief is often deep, their resentment justified, their brokenness beyond anything they thought they could ever endure.

It is easy for any of these women to fall into the trap of thinking themselves to be all good and the unfaithful husband all bad. Who wouldn't? It's a natural reaction. But as time and healing occur, these betrayed women must begin to look realistically at their own lives. They did not cause the unfaithfulness, but they were not perfect either. Everyone makes mistakes. The more the betrayed begin to see their own flaws, the more likely they are to be willing to move toward forgiveness and attempt steps that might heal the relationship. This might be the most difficult thing they ever attempt. It also might be the thing that frees them from a life of bitterness, anger, and isolation.

Even when we recognize our sins and deal with them, we often find it hard to forgive ourselves. In fact, this is often one reason we find it so hard to forgive others. Believe it or not, you are the most difficult person you have to forgive. You may try to let go of the guilt and accept God's grace, but your conscience—that often troublesome and legalistic intruder—fails to get the message and continues to prod you, making self-forgiveness a real chore.

Self-forgiveness comes much easier when you realize that God's grace is free and complete. And one of the best ways to know you are forgiven is to forgive others. In forgiving others you can see the forgiveness of God more clearly, simply because you become an enactor and reflector of it. God's character flows through you. Modeling his grace and forgiveness allows you to see the process from the inside and understand up close and personal what God has done for you.

Seeking Forgiveness through Confession

If you are the spouse who has committed an offense, then your role in restoring the relationship is to seek forgiveness. It is important that you feel true remorse and contrition for the pain you have caused and that you convey those feelings clearly to your mate. You must be willing to make a commitment to him or her that you will not repeat the hurtful behavior. If there are consequences to be borne as a result of the behavior, be ready and willing to bear them, whatever the cost. If your mate has trouble forgiving you, be patient. Remember that forgiveness often takes time, and the deeper the hurt, the more time it may take. In fact, forgiveness may not come until you have taken positive steps to rebuild trust.

Many times the missing element in receiving forgiveness is restitution. It is one thing for a gambling addict to come home and say, "Honey, I lost my job and I gambled away all of our retirement. Will you please forgive me?" It's quite another for him to make restitution: "I can't tell you how sorry I am for all I've done. I pledge to you that I will join Gamblers Anonymous and attend regularly. Tomorrow I promise to get up, put on my coat and tie, and start looking for work. If I must work three jobs, I'll do it. I will put my bass boat up for sale immediately. I'll let you be in charge of the finances from now on. We can go to counseling together and start our healing." An approach such as this is not perfect; confession and restitution doesn't undo the damage or solve all the problems. But if it's sincere, it is the right kind of start in seeking true forgiveness.

When confessing and seeking forgiveness, it is important that you take full responsibility for your own actions. Confessing a wrong and asking forgiveness means expressing remorse, and if your remorse is genuine, you will not justify your action with excuses. If you claim an excusable reason for the hurt you inflicted, then your confession and apology is meaningless. To accompany your apology with an excuse is an illegitimate attempt to justify the hurtful action. You are failing to take full responsibility, putting the blame on another person or on circumstance.

This is why you should avoid "if-but" apologies. They are self-justifying. "I'm sorry *if* I offended you, *but* you need to understand that I was under extreme stress at the time." In other words, it was not really my fault and you should not have been offended because you should understand that I had a valid excuse for doing what I did. "I'm sorry *if* your feelings got hurt, *but* I did not think you would be so sensitive." In other words, it was your fault that my words hurt you, not mine. I was just being myself. You need to develop thicker skin so I won't have to mind my tongue. An "if-but" apology is not really a confession; it's an evasion.

A real confession accepts full responsibility: "I was wrong. I have no excuse for what I did. I was being selfish and did not consider you as I should have. I am very sorry. I promise to make a sincere attempt to do better in the future. Please forgive me."

Related to this principle is the need to be quick to forgive the little things that happen daily in a marriage. We are all fallen creatures who do not always manage our emotions and responses perfectly, and little offenses of no real consequence are sure to be a part of daily life. While you should not blame your offenses against your mate on his or her sensitivity, neither should you let the other's momentary lapse drive a wedge into the relationship. If he is a little snappish when he is struggling to connect a new U-trap under a leaky sink, don't require an apology or a confession. Just let it roll off. He's not upset with you; he's upset with that confounded U-trap or a wrench that keeps slipping or his fumbling hands. Forgive without being asked. If she claims (or has) a headache when you are eager for a romp in the bed, don't pout for the next three days. Forgive her without requiring an apology. Let it roll off. Pouting or complaining is not an effective aphrodisiac likely to make her more eager for the bedroom on the following night.

In a relationship as close as marriage where you are with each other every day for hours at a time, both of you should lower your sensitivity to hurt. Minor everyday failures are sure to happen—a snappish word, forgetting to pick up the cleaning, a failure to compliment a hairdo, overcooking the casserole. Instead of taking offense, be ready to extend grace.

The Critical Importance of Forgiveness

Forgiveness is one of the most critical elements in any relationship. We are all sinners, and we all hurt others. The closer the relationship, the more opportunities for hurt. That is why forgiveness is a key element in binding together a man and woman in marriage.

You should forgive your mate simply because you love him or her. That is why God forgave you, and that alone is reason enough to forgive each other. It will do untold good to your marriage if you and your mate will memorize and practice the plea of the apostle Paul in his letter to the Ephesians: "Be kind to one another, tenderhearted, forgiving one another, even as God in Christ forgave you" (Ephesians 4:32 NKJV).

Choose to forgive your spouse and extend grace to him or her every day. Express an attitude of grace in what you do and how you interact. The more ways you can create to express your attitude of grace, the stronger your marriage will be!

7

THINGS TO DO IF YOUR SPOUSE
Does Not Express Grace and Forgiveness

- Be sure you have expressed your need to feel your spouse's grace on a daily basis.

- Discuss what things are in the past that both of you have done that are still affecting the relationship today.

- Talk about ways you can meet your spouse's needs in other areas as well as his or her need to feel your grace and acceptance.

- Take responsibility for your mistakes and failures and do whatever it takes for your spouse to know you have.

- Always go beyond saying you are sorry for something that is a repeated offense and be willing to get help if needed.

- In a negative relationship where all your faults and flaws are pointed out and there is little or no grace expressed, you need tremendous support from family, friends, and perhaps a professional counselor and pastor.

- In addition to support, seek professional help so that a long-term strategy can be developed and maintained.

11

[START AFFIRMING]
YOUR MATE'S STRENGTHS

To watch a short video on this subject, go to
7MinuteMarriageSolution.com/11

How much time do you spend criticizing the behavior of your spouse, and how much do you spend affirming his or her strengths? The marriage that makes it is on a journey of acceptance and affirmation. The sooner you get there, the better. Accepting your mate's weaknesses while affirming his or her strengths is one of the requirements of a lasting and meaningful relationship. When you travel toward acceptance and affirmation, you are fleeing from the impossible ideal and into the real. You are discontinuing the rejection of all things that don't meet your expectations. You are offering the grace God has given you to the person you love. You are freed from being disappointed about your spouse's flaws—instead, you are able to identify and appreciate your spouse's good qualities.

> THE MORE YOU ACCEPT THE OTHER PERSON,
> THE MORE LIKELY IT IS THAT YOUR MATE WILL
> TRANSFORM INTO THE BEST HE OR SHE CAN BE.

Acceptance does more than just liberate you from the disappointment of unmet expectations. It also frees your mate to transform. That's right. The more you accept the other person, the more likely it is that your mate will transform into the best he or she can be. Note that you are not trying to change your spouse (we covered that in chapter 4). But your acceptance allows your mate the freedom to try new attitudes and behaviors rather than just defend the way he or she has been living. And as you begin to appreciate and affirm your spouse's positive qualities, you free him to cast off some bad habits as he grows into his fullest potential. If you cannot call yourself a person of radical acceptance and affirmation, I invite you to incorporate this liberating concept into your life and into your marriage.

Dealing with Real Flaws

In all marriages, unsuspected defects, faults, idiosyncrasies, and annoying behaviors show up after the vows are spoken. These flaws vary from trivial to mountainous. Some don't cook well. Some can't hammer any nail but their thumbnail. Some people don't communicate enough. Some communicate too much. Some are not romantic; others are not realistic. Some spend too much; others pinch a penny until it squeals. Some are sloppy; some are neatniks. Some even have serious habits of deceit or secrecy.

Of course, many of our flaws are not merely innocent differences or the result of our gender or background, as discussed in chapter 1. Instead, they are real faults of varying levels of seriousness. So how should married couples treat these real flaws? There are two answers, depending on what the flaw is. I'll deal first with the most serious problems.

As discussed in chapter 6, acceptance does not include abusive, addictive, or other destructive behaviors that require confrontation or intervention. These are behaviors that simply cannot be tolerated. Marital unfaithfulness or physical, mental, or psychological abuse must not be tolerated. Neither should illegal behaviors or addictions like alcohol, drugs, gambling, or pornography.

In a counseling session, one young woman told me what happened when she came out of the bathroom on her wedding night eager to slip into bed with her new husband. He was waiting for her, but to her shock, he was smoking a joint. She stopped immediately, covered herself with a robe, and said, "I never saw you smoking marijuana before, and I am not going to put up with it now. I will not be married to this behavior. Either you put that thing away and vow never to do it again or I'm walking out of here right now, and you can tell your friends that you couldn't even satisfy your new wife for one night." She was unwilling to accept the behavior but willing to accept the person if he separated himself from the behavior.

Committing a serious sin or being caught in an addiction doesn't mean your husband or wife is an all-out bad person—just a person who has made a mistake. The mistake is only one small part of who he or she is. You must not accept the behavior, but you must accept the person who separates himself from the behavior.

Dealing with Your Mate's Lesser Faults

How should couples deal with the less damaging flaws we have all picked up or acquired in our past—flaws that don't really harm us or our mates, but act as irritants or inconveniences, or cause embarrassment or frustration? The answer: deal with them in the same way you deal with your innocent or inherent differences. Accept them. Maybe he is sloppy, leaving clothes strewn about, not helping with housework, or leaving dishes and glasses wherever he uses them. Maybe she is habitually late, causing you to miss the first minutes of most movies, concerts, and church services. You can probably add a few things to this list yourself.

THE WAY OF LOVE, THE WAY OF COMMITMENT,
AND THE WAY OF CHRIST IS TO ACCEPT
THE FLAWS AND WEAKNESSES OF YOUR
MATE AND LOVE IN SPITE OF THEM.

Running away is the selfish way out. The coward's way. But the way of love, the way of commitment, and the way of Christ is to accept the flaws and weaknesses of your mate and love in spite of them. Let's talk about how this works.

Marriage is a process of moving out of idealization of the other person to acceptance of all that he or she is and does. The man you married is not the prince you thought he was. The woman you married is not a combination of your mom and a French courtesan. Acceptance involves a process of absorbing this shock of reality and dealing with it. It's actually a process of grieving the loss of the person you thought you married and accepting the reality of the one you did. Every day is an exercise in acceptance. Fortunately in every husband and wife reside great attributes that counterbalance the negatives in the person you accept and love.

The Rewards of Affirmation

You married your mate because you saw great attributes in that person, and you knew you could love someone like that forever. Then you found that along with those lovable attributes came a few unpleasant surprises. What you must realize is that the person you married is a whole package. The desirable and undesirable traits are enmeshed with each other. When you buy the package you accept both the good and the bad; you don't try to remake your mate to fit your own ideal. Instead of focusing on your spouse's flaws by judging or insisting that your mate meet your standards, free your mate to be herself by affirming her strengths. Help your mate to be comfortable in his own skin without having to worry that he's being continually monitored for acceptability.

I believe that deep inside, you want those differences much more than you realize. What you perceive as a flaw likely adds a dimension to your life that you would miss if you married a clone of yourself. Living with someone just like yourself might be more harmonious, but it would also be more boring. How would you experience new perspectives, new ways of thinking, new surprises? Marrying someone who is totally different may bring on more frustrations, but it's also a lot more fun. As the French say, *"Vive la différence!"*

Affirming your mate's strengths does not mean you have to like everything about your mate. That would certainly be a modern-day miracle.

Sometimes she will drive you crazy. Sometimes he will make you want to scream and pull out your hair—or his. But each of you must realize that you also take a lot of putting up with. To receive acceptance and affirmation, you must give acceptance and affirmation. Couples who learn to accept one another as they are find enormous strength for binding their marriage, because it's a marriage built on truth instead of fantasy. This love accepts the flaws but penetrates beyond them and chooses to focus on the positive. Affirming your mate's strengths in spite of his flaws is a sign of mature love.

AFFIRMING YOUR MATE'S STRENGTHS IN SPITE OF HIS FLAWS IS A SIGN OF MATURE LOVE.

We all have a deep need to have someone who loves us for who we really are. We want someone we can be with without fear of rejection or disapproval. We want someone for whom we don't have to perform in a certain way to earn love. We all want to feel secure that our mate's love is simply there for us and will always be there even when we mess up terribly. We want the kind of love the apostle Paul wrote about when he said, "Love suffers long and is kind; love . . . bears all things, believes all things, hopes all things, endures all things" (1 Corinthians 13:4–7 NKJV). If you will continue to read, I will help you get to that place of love where much is accepted and much is overlooked.

Dr. Jim Bradford, general secretary of the Assemblies of God, tells a story about the "Fault Box." A wife was utterly disgruntled with her husband's abundant flaws and sloppy habits. She had tried to get him to quit leaving his socks strewn about the floor, to quit messing up the kitchen counter with peanut butter, and to correct several other irritating habits. Nothing worked. He persisted in his wayward ways until she decided she had to take more effective steps.

So she set up a box in the kitchen with a slot in the top and labeled it the "Fault Box." She told her husband to write down her faults as he encountered them and drop them into that box. She would do the same, and in thirty days they would open the box and each would read the faults the other had noted.

Over the next thirty days she dropped quite a number of notes into the box. She noticed her husband doing the same. Finally, at the end of the month she called him in, and they sat down to see what each had put in the box. He read the ones she had written first. Each note listed one of his faults—the sloppy habits, the messy counter, and several other failures.

When it was her turn, she unfolded the first note. It said, simply, "I love you." She went to the second note. Same message: "I love you." She went to the third, the fourth, and all the rest. All bore she same message: "I love you."

The humbled wife learned something vitally important that day. Each time her husband had noticed one of her faults, instead of listing it he wrote what was more important than the fault itself: his love for her. He covered her faults with his love.[1] It's what the apostle Peter urges us to do: "Above all things have fervent love for one another, for 'love will cover a multitude of sins'" (1 Peter 4:8 NKJV).

It's what we call grace. Just as God in his grace covers our sins with his love, we have the privilege of covering the sins and flaws of our mate with our own love. Marriage gives us a perfect way to become more Christlike— a way of exercising and passing on the same kind of grace he gives to us. It is one more opportunity God gives us to reflect the nature of Christ and to love as he does.

Try to keep this wonderful verse in mind: "Therefore accept each other just as Christ has accepted you so that God will be given glory" (Romans 15:7).

THINGS TO DO IF YOUR SPOUSE
Does Not Affirm Your Strengths

- Be sure that you are not critical of your spouse and you provide the very affirmation you are looking for.

- Try to engage in a conversation to determine if there is some major issue that has not been resolved that is leading to the focus on so many minor issues.

- Explore if there is something that you do that reminds your spouse of another who was hurtful.

- Examine yourself and try to determine what is the toughest thing about you to embrace and develop a plan to improve in that area.

- Ask your spouse to pick one area where you could improve and to tell you one area where you are strong.

- Work with a counselor on your own to grow and develop so that the criticism or lack of acceptance is easier to bear and is seen more as a problem with your spouse than something you can fix by changing.

- Refuse to counter any criticism with another criticism back.

$\big[$ START SPENDING $\big]$
MONEY RESPONSIBLY

To watch a short video on this subject, go to
7MinuteMarriageSolution.com/12

Boom! That is what I hope you feel from reading this chapter. It is what I felt when I woke up, saw the reality of my financial life, and started making the changes I needed to make. And I was never the same. The boom went off in my head when I realized I had been soothing the bruising of my soul by spending money. I had been abandoned and betrayed and I was in pain. The spending became my comfort food to numb the pain. Then the depression I was in grew worse because of the debt. I realized I just might die one day and leave my wife in debt. So the extravagant spending stopped, the downsizing started, we attended a financial seminar, and everything everyone had ever said about the freedom of getting out of debt proved true. I hope the boom will go off in your head before it is too late. I hope something in the following pages will explode in front of you, and when the dust clears you will have clarity. Clarity in the area of finances can lead you and your spouse to security and satisfaction that will benefit you for years to come.

Brad and Cheryl, now in midlife and financially comfortable, remember well their first two years of marriage. They were still in college, both working part time earning minimum wage, and money was scarce as icicles in July. Often they ran out of funds before payday. Desperately needing a couple of gallons of gas or a can of beans, they would embark on a quest for cash, scrounging about in furniture drawers, under chairs and sofa cushions and car seats looking for change that might have fallen out of pockets. Or they went on forays along highways picking up aluminum cans and cashing them in.

Today they remember those times fondly. They laugh at the poverty of their early years and claim they lived solely on love. But their memory has done a bit of selective editing. They have forgotten that at the time, their financial struggles were anything but funny.

A lot of couples middle-aged or older are not laughing at the poverty of their younger days because they are still living in those days. They never pulled out of the financial nosedive they faced early in marriage. They find themselves either crashing in financial ruin or barely managing to stay aloft while skimming the crags and treetops, weighted down by heavy debt and out-of-control spending. As a result, money and finances run neck-and-neck with sex as the number-one causes of relational friction in marriage.

Most couples face financial difficulty because they exercise little or no planning or discipline regarding the use of their money. If you want to get out of the stressful cycle of financial strain . . .

- *You may have some tough choices to make.* Save rather than spend. Stay rather than go. Say no rather than yes.
- *You may have some tough habits to break.* Impulse buying. Eating out too often. Relying on plastic. Buying without comparing.
- *You may have some false assumptions to give up.* Everything won't necessarily work according to your financial plan. Faith in God cannot replace financial responsibility. Your investments may not always pay.
- *You may have some acts to surrender or to commit.* Should you surrender the credit cards? Should you commit to a budget? Should the two of you get on the same page financially?

If you are dealing with any of these issues about money, this chapter will give you clarity regarding financial responsibility in your marriage.

Common Causes of Financial Conflict

John D. Rockefeller was the first American billionaire. A reporter once asked him, "How much money is enough?" He answered, "Just a little bit more."

That's how we all tend to think, isn't it? *If I had just a little bit more money, a few more things, a little better home, a little newer car, a few more toys, then I would really be happy.* We've heard all our lives that money can't buy happiness, but we don't live like we really believe it. As one wag said, "Money may not buy happiness, but it sure can make unhappiness a lot more comfortable."

Most of us have heard all of our lives that money can't buy happiness. A lot of studies have been done that prove it. But we all think we are the exception or that whether or not it will make us happy, we want as much of it as we can get.

THE REAL PROBLEM IS THEIR UNREALISTIC
EXPECTATIONS, WHICH MEANS THEY DON'T HAVE
ENOUGH MONEY TO BUY EVERYTHING THEY WANT.

Most couples think just like Mr. Rockefeller. They are convinced their money problems would be solved if they had just a little bit more. That is seldom true. The real problem is their unrealistic expectations, which means they don't have enough money to buy everything they want.

As I write this, the US economy is in a recession and shaky as Jell-O. But people still expect to have all the bells and whistles of comfort, entertainment, and recreation—a large house, fine furniture, seventy-inch HD-TVs in the den and bedroom, a new SUV, motorcycle, ski boat, and cruise vacations. Usually they either buy these things on credit, which causes conflict, or they feel deprived, which causes conflict.

If you tend to spend beyond your income, it may be worthwhile to search for the underlying reasons. One common reason is insecurity. You may have been raised in a financially strapped home, and you could not dress as well as your peers or afford the extras they took for granted. Now that you have a little money, you tend to indulge all those things you were previously denied.

You may overspend because you have an unwritten list of accumulated wants that you will buy "when I can afford it." Then when you do get a little extra overtime cash or a tax refund, the entire amount goes to purchasing those wants instead of building a reserve. Spending gives you a rush of freedom from the restraints of having to scrimp.

Many people spend to be like their peers. This is another form of insecurity—a misguided way of saying to others, "See, I'm just as good as you are. I have value." That is unmitigated pride at work in your life. If you have a problem with uncontrolled overspending, a candid, objective examination of your past or your motives could do much to curb the problem.

Conflict also arises when either spouse spends money secretly. He wants a new hunting rifle. She wants a new dining table. She can't see why he needs another rifle, and he can't see anything wrong with their present table. They don't have the funds for either, so without consulting the other each makes his or her desired purchase. The pattern repeats a few times, money becomes tight, bills go unpaid, and each spouse blames the other for their overstretched budget.

Sometimes the true source of the conflict over finances may not really be about money. One spouse may harbor hurt or resentment in some other area that has not been dealt with. The emotions driven by this deeper hurt may emerge in money disagreements and escalate the conflict to new levels.

My goal in this chapter is simple. I want to help you and your spouse avoid the relational iceberg of financial conflict by getting on the same page financially. I want to help you explore the monetary problems couples tend to have so you can work together to solve them. To this end, I will give you an overview of common wisdom that you can begin applying to your own finances.

Yours, Mine, or Ours?

When both the husband and wife earn incomes, the question arises as to who controls the money. In too many homes today, the husband and wife maintain separate bank accounts. I strongly discourage this arrangement because it erodes oneness, leading to separateness in other areas and setting up the couple for power struggles.

While maintaining separate accounts might seem to solve some financial conflict problems by diminishing the need for mutual planning and accountability, it creates other problems. One is inequity. When one income is notably smaller than the other, the spouse with the lesser income may feel like the junior partner in the relationship or suffer a sense of deprivation or inferiority.

Another problem with separate accounts arises when one spouse is financially responsible and the other is not. Chad and Doris were both teachers earning similar incomes. Being a thoroughly postmodern couple, they chose to keep separate bank accounts and share expenses evenly. But Chad had a spending problem, and he consistently blew his paycheck on shop equipment, fishing tackle, golfing, or electronic gadgets. He was usually broke a week before the next check arrived. This meant Doris had to pay most of the bills and pick up the tabs when they ate out, as they typically did during the school year.

You and your mate cannot be truly one as long as you maintain separate finances. Incomes should be merged and managed together. Separate discretionary spending funds within the shared account (a concept I will address below) may sometimes be in order. But that should be the limit of separateness. A shared bank account requires faith and trust in each other. But that is a good thing for your marriage.

Plan a Budget Together

Many couple's budget problems are due to a failure to communicate to each other their financial priorities. Larry loves to build and repair computers and he's very good at it. He heads up the IT department for a large company, but he has always dreamed of having his own computer repair and consulting business. Every payday he socks away a few dollars toward accomplishing that dream. His wife, Janie, on the other hand, has dreams of redoing her home and yard. Every payday she buys paint, curtains, or shrubs and flowers. When money runs short for bills, both are upset because neither can understand where it all goes.

COMMUNICATE TO EACH OTHER HOPES AND
EXPECTATIONS THAT INVOLVE MONEY AND
MAKE A BUDGET THAT ACCOMMODATES
BOTH NECESSITIES AND DREAMS.

Like many married couples, Larry and Janie are frustrated because they have never discussed goals that involve the use of money. They have never spoken of budgeting—how to regulate spending to be sure they have money for their goals and needs. The answer is to make it a priority to communicate to each other hopes and expectations that involve money and make a budget that accommodates both necessities and dreams.

Financial matters can get touchy, and it's not uncommon for either mate to be reluctant to discuss them. But there are ways to encourage a husband or wife to do it. Gary Smalley suggests that the wife use word pictures to engage a reluctant husband: "Honey, when you blow off looking at these bills with me and I have to deal with the collectors alone, it makes me feel the same way as I would if I were kidnapped right in front of you and you did nothing to protect me."[1] Ouch! Such a picture is sure to get a caring husband's attention.

Christian financial expert Dave Ramsey has advice for persuading a reluctant wife to engage in financial planning: "Husbands, when you're trying to get your wife onboard, remember that she is wired for relationships and security. Asking her a question such as, 'How would it feel if we had ten thousand dollars in savings just for emergencies?' will get her attention." Ramsey then offers a second approach to punch her relational button: "Ninety-seven percent of women surveyed said they would like more communication in marriage. So what if you said, 'Honey, I was reading about how if we spent a few minutes a week working on a budget together, it would increase our communication in every area and ultimately create more intimacy and unity. Would you like to try that?' I'm willing to bet you won't need to say much more."[2]

After communicating your goals, the next step is to establish a budget designed to accomplish them. You should do this together or one of you could draft the budget for the two of you to go over to ensure agreement. The result should be a realistically achievable spending plan.

This initial budgeting should include a fund for emergencies. Murphy's Law always hovers, ready to smash your budget with an auto transmission going out or a home air conditioner blowing a compressor. If these emergencies pile up, or if they occur before your fund is large enough to cover them, you should agree up front on a plan B, which may include borrowing or drawing funds from regular savings.

You also need an up-front plan for windfall income, such as bequests, gifts, tax refunds, and so on. Without a plan such money usually gets blown away in the wind of the I've-scrimped-so-long-I-deserve-to-splurge syndrome. Agree in advance whether extra money will go to a fund within the budget, be shared discretionary money, or go to your church or a charity.

Your budget needs to include not only a plan for your immediate income and outflow; it should also address long-range goals and needs. Crown Financial Ministries encourages spouses to discuss long-term financial goals: "This would include not only children's college educations, children's marriages, and retirement, but also what to do in the event that one spouse dies before the other."[3]

Budgeting means bookkeeping. Without managing and tracking your income and outflow, your budget will quickly get out of hand. One of you must be designated to manage your finances—paying the bills, updating the checkbook, maintaining records, and allocating funds according to the plan.

This must not be a financial takeover! Both should agree on which of you will manage the budget, and it should generally be the one who is best at math.

Though only one spouse manages the budget, both need to be savvy about everything in it. Both should know where the accounts and investments are located. And while I'm in the neighborhood, I'll throw in a bit of related advice at no extra charge: both of you must know the location of important papers such as insurance policies, property deeds, car titles, marriage license, wills, account numbers, the key to the lockbox, and so on.

Be Mutually Accountable

Once a budget is agreed to, both you and your mate must determine to be dependable and trustworthy in sticking to it. One step that will help is an ironclad pact that there will be no major purchases without mutual agreement between the two of you.

The potential difficulty in this rule is, of course, that the two of you will not always want the same things. When he wants a new fishing boat and she wants a new car, a calm and rational discussion is in order, or maybe a little attitude adjustment on the part of each (see chapter 7). It's possible that both expenditures can be accommodated if they are made one at a time. Then the only item for discussion is who goes first.

Some financial advisers recommend that if the budget allows for discretionary spending—that is, if there is money left over after meeting all the necessary expenses and savings allocations—each spouse can have his and her own luxury spending fund within the account. While all other spending requires accountability, money in the spouse's own luxury fund does not. No matter how unnecessary one spouse may consider the other's purchase—her hundred-dollar fitness pants or his combination cell phone and razor—each can spend freely from his or her fund with no questions asked and no snide comments.

If you violate any principle of the budget, overspending in some area or making a major purchase the other didn't agree to, that money should be docked from your luxury spending fund.

Slaying the Dragon of Debt

In today's consumer economy, we are continually urged to buy-buy-buy. You want a Lexus but you have a Chevy budget? No problem. Just sign this twenty-seven-page loan agreement promising lifetime indenture and your firstborn and you can park it in your garage today. You want a houseful of new furniture, jet skis, trail bikes, or a Caribbean cruise but you only have $28.19 in your savings account? No big deal. Just swipe one of your thirteen credit cards and it's yours right now.

Americans have been doing this for decades, and the result is an unprecedented nationwide load of personal debt amounting to 2.5 trillion dollars as of December 2011. The average household debt on credit cards alone is almost $16,000 per family.[4] Many of these households have several cards, all with outstanding balances, and making the minimum payments is one of their major monthly expenses.

I've heard financial advisers urge couples to cut up their credit cards. But in today's culture that is not always possible. You need credit cards for most online commerce, purchasing airline tickets, and renting cars. But one or two cards are enough. So make it a habit to shred all those credit-card offers that clog your mailbox. To keep your card debt from getting out of hand, resolve to pay off the balance monthly, if possible, and leave only enough debt on the card to keep it active. Set a debt limit, and keep it low.

I realize that few couples can pay cash for everything they need, especially homes and cars. That's why we have mortgage companies and banks. Taking on a debt for a house—and usually for an automobile—is unavoidable for most couples. The common mistake, however, is in buying more house or car than your budget can sustain. When the monthly payments begin to loom, the budget can strain to the breaking point.

While most people see financing a car as unavoidable (and in many cases it is), the majority of car purchases are made long before they need to be. Glenn and Carrie's family sedan was six years old, and within the past year they had to replace the water pump, fix the alternator, and have the brake drums turned. Glenn figured it was time to trade, so he paid a visit to a local dealership.

It didn't take but a whiff of the new-car smell before he was drooling over a sparkling new SUV calling to him from the showroom. It had power everything, front and back air conditioning, a push-button sunroof, a built-in DVD player, and electric seat warmers. He got a pencil and gerrymandered the budget to accommodate the payments and presented the idea to Carrie.

She didn't warm to the purchase. She reminded Glenn of their teenage daughter's need for braces and all the costs involved with their son heading for college in the fall. Glenn was disappointed, but he didn't put up a fight because he knew she was right. When he actually compared the cost of the new car to maintaining the old one, he had to admit the purchase didn't make budgetary sense. New car payments for one year were quadruple the cost of last year's repairs on their present car. Being of sound mind, he realized his real problem was that driving his old car was not as cool or satisfying as driving a new one. He chucked his figures in the trash and actually let out a sigh of relief at not having to face the strain of an overextended budget.

Even when it does come time for Glenn to trade, buying a fairly recent model, vetted used car is much more economically efficient than absorbing the enormous depreciation that occurs the moment you drive a new one off the lot. And he can get that new-car smell with a little aroma tablet from his local carwash.

———————

TO AVOID FINANCIAL DISASTER, YOU MUST
CLOSE YOUR EARS TO THE SIREN VOICES OF
GOVERNMENT AND ALLURING TV COMMERCIALS
URGING YOU TO SPEND YOUR WAY TO PROSPERITY.

———————

To avoid financial disaster, you must close your ears to the siren voices of government and alluring TV commercials urging you to spend your way to prosperity and swipe your card at every store in town. Lead yourself not into temptation. If you love watching the specials on the Home Shopping or QVC networks, reprogram your remote to skip those channels.

Many people love to go shopping even if they have no need to buy anything. The daughter of a friend of mine shops so much that someone gave her a large pin-on button reading, "I shop, therefore I am." Going shopping almost always results in a purchase, and it's a subtle snare that can quickly cause debt to soar. If you love to shop, know your spending limit and stick to it.

If you are already deeply in debt, stop all discretionary spending and devote those funds to paying off your debt. If you cannot adjust your budget to do this, then contact one of the many services that offer help and budgetary advice for families with unmanageable debt.

Force Yourselves to Save

As a result of our national buying binge, per capita savings are at their lowest point in America's history. This means many families with two wage earners and above-average incomes are living paycheck to paycheck, struggling with debt, and failing to save. They are highly vulnerable to financial disaster because they have no financial cushion to break their fall.

Saving is a necessary factor in responsible budgeting. Saving enables you to handle emergencies that would otherwise blow your budget to smithereens. Saving prepares you for retirement when your income will be lower or nonexistent. It enables you to make large purchases without going into debt. And it enables you to accumulate funds for your children's education.

There are many ways to save. Among these are IRAs, 401(k)s, CDs, US Treasury notes, and savings accounts. I recommend that you consult a financial adviser to determine which is best for you. Remember that investments are not savings. Investments should be considered risks to be made only out of discretionary funds. Never invest more than you can afford to lose.

If you don't save because you lack the discipline, own up to it and find a solution. One solution is automatic payroll deduction by your employer to a program such as a 401(k) account. Another is to automatically split your paycheck deposit, putting a preplanned percentage into savings before you ever touch any of the money. Using these methods, your savings, like your tax deduction, comes out of money you never see and thus you don't miss it.

The golden rule that enables saving is always to spend less than you earn. That is the real way to build financial security. Most people today tend to spend just a little more than they earn, which means their budget is always expanding like hot air in a balloon and putting increasing pressure on their income. If your income is low, that simply means your lifestyle choices need to be scaled to fit what you make. Your dream house, luxury car, and updated entertainment center may have to wait, but your savings should continue. The reason most people fail to save is that they have been conditioned to mistake extras for necessities.

One good way to balance responsible spending and saving is to buy wisely. Compare prices, look for sales. Thrift stores and consignment shops often have good bargains on clothing or furniture that appear to be new. Carolyn MacInnes offers a great list of practical money-saving tips on the Focus on the Family website.[5]

Whose Money Is It, Anyway?

As you work with your family finances, it is imperative that you remember whose money you're dealing with. As Christians, we understand that everything in this universe belongs to God, and that includes your money. Christ made this principle clear in the parable of the bags of gold in Matthew 25. As you remember, a businessman gave three servants a certain number of bags of gold to care for individually while he went away on a journey. When he returned, he required each servant to account for how he had used the money entrusted to him.

It's the same with us. God entrusts to each of us however much money he thinks we can handle, and he will demand an accounting as to whether we used it well or poorly. This does not necessarily mean just your tithe; it covers the whole gamut of how you handle money. Do you squander it on yourself or blow it on meaningless frivolities? Or do you use it to help others or to foster solid values in your life and that of your family?

Financial responsibility before God includes tithing. Throughout biblical history tithing has been required of God's people. Abraham tithed to the priest-king Melchizedek (Genesis 14:18–20). God commanded Israel to tithe (Leviticus 27:30). The prophet Malachi told Israel that by withholding their tithes, they were robbing God, which would result in disaster (3:8–9). On the other hand, he promised overflowing blessings if they tithed: "'Test me in this,' says the LORD Almighty, 'and see if I will not throw open the floodgates of heaven and pour out so much blessing that there will not be room enough to store it'" (v. 10 NIV).

We know this promise is for us as well, for Christ himself affirmed the principle: "Give, and it will be given to you. A good measure, pressed down, shaken together and running over, will be poured into your lap. For with the measure you use, it will be measured to you" (Luke 6:38 NIV).

We are told to tithe not because God needs the money. He owns the universe! It's because we need to give. Giving shows our dedication to God and curbs our natural tendency toward selfishness. It also reminds us of our total dependence on God for everything we have and gives us a way to acknowledge it and show our gratitude. The resulting rewards he promises are merely his way of expressing his approval for our being responsible.

WITH PRAYER AND PLANNING, YOU AND YOUR
SPOUSE CAN BE ON THE SAME PAGE FINANCIALLY.

With prayer and planning, you and your spouse can be on the same page financially. You can have unified clarity concerning your use of money. You can give up self-reliance or irresponsible presumption upon God and be set free—financially free. What a way to live!

THINGS TO DO IF YOUR SPOUSE
Doesn't Spend Money Responsibly

- Request that the two of you talk to a financial counselor or adviser from a ministry like Crown Financial Ministries.

- Request marital counseling in an effort to build connection between the two of you that will help in resolving financial issues and all others.

- Develop a budget and be generous with the discretionary spending category for your spouse, showing that it might be easier to live within a budget than expected.

- Request the two of you attend a financial seminar that might bring new insights to your spouse.

- Spend time talking to your spouse about your dreams, hopes, and desires of what life would be like in twenty years. Paint a picture of what a financially free future looks like and show how much money will be needed to get to that future.

- Evaluate your approach to finances to ensure you are not motivated by a need to control versus a desire for future financial freedom.

- If impulsive spending threatens financial stability for you, you may have to take a drastic measure of legal separation of finances. (This is only called for in extreme cases.)

13

[START PRACTICING]
YOUR LIFETIME VOWS

To watch a short video on this subject, go to
7MinuteMarriageSolution.com/13

What do you do when your spouse is unfaithful? Do you stay or do you go? Just a few days ago I was talking to a man whose wife had broken their wedding vows. Most men don't keep their wedding vows after the wife has broken hers, but this exceptional man did. He realized he was not a perfect husband, and he wondered whether he might have done things that contributed to her unfaithfulness. He chose not to divorce her as long as the two of them got help for their problems.

But after he made that decision, the plot thickened. A test revealed that she was pregnant by another man. But this man of character still did not waver in his commitment. He had made a vow to love her when they married, and he was determined to do what he said he would do. When the baby was born he adopted her and loved her as his own. He made her a vow that he would be her father no matter what. Now that was a man who understood what it means to keep a vow!

Today we tend to use the word *promise* more than *vow*, but they are the same thing: a binding commitment to do what you say you will do. When a person makes a vow, he gives his word, and when he gives his word, his integrity is on the line. A person's word is closely identified with the person himself. His word reveals his character and tells us who he is. The apostle John asserts this fact most dramatically in the first words of his gospel where he identifies Jesus as the Word of God—the emanation or expression of God that reveals God's character.

This binding connection between a person and his word is why God looks upon a vow as an extremely serious thing. As Moses writes, "When a man makes a vow to the LORD or takes an oath to obligate himself by a pledge, he must not break his word but must do everything he said" (Numbers 30:2 NIV).

GOD LOOKS UPON A VOW AS AN
EXTREMELY SERIOUS THING.

Obviously the people of the Bible understood the high seriousness of a vow and acted accordingly. Today we have largely lost that awareness. I presume that most people who make promises intend to keep them. But if keeping a promise becomes inconvenient or difficult, all too many feel justified in breaking it.

As we all know, politicians provide the model for promise-breaking. Vows to them seem to be like your mother's piecrusts: easily made, easily broken. Most pundits believe that President George H. W. Bush lost his bid for reelection because he reneged on a particularly important campaign promise. During the 1988 campaign he famously promised, "Read my lips: no new taxes." When he subsequently agreed to raise taxes, the broken promise became his downfall in the 1992 election.

I suspect that today married couples have overtaken politicians as the worst vow-breakers. Nowhere is today's lax attitude toward vows more evident than in marriages. Couples stand before a minister clasping each other's hands and vow to love each other "in sickness and in health, for better or for worse, till death do us part." It is a solemn promise, a lifetime commitment before God and witnesses that they will remain faithful and true to each other throughout their lives. But any inconvenience, any conflict, any problem, any loss of attractiveness or romantic feeling, or any appealing man or woman on the other side of the fence often causes either partner to renege on the vow and break up the marriage.

Four Causes of Broken Wedding Vows

There may be a thousand excuses for breaking wedding vows, but God condones only two as valid reasons: abandonment and adultery. In cases of unfaithfulness, the offended party is justified in leaving the marriage because the other person broke the vow (Matthew 19:8–9). This frees the innocent party from adhering to it.

The only other justifiable divorce situation detailed in Scripture is when a spouse who is an unbeliever abandons the believing spouse (1 Corinthians 7:14–15). These are the exceptions where divorce can be initiated on biblical grounds. In every other situation the believer is admonished to seek a solution to the problem rather than to divorce.

Aside from unfaithfulness, however, I believe about 99.9 percent of broken marriage vows stem in some way from sheer selfishness. The marriage turns out not to be what you wanted. It's harder than you expected, not as exciting, it cramps your style, it ties you down, it requires too much give and take, your mate has flaws you didn't expect, or you don't get along very well.

Over the years I have found that most of this selfishness falls under one or more of the following four categories—routine, regret, rule-breaking, or risky choices. Let's explore these categories one by one.

ROUTINE

Like in the old Johnny Cash/June Carter song "Jackson," Eddie and Kristi were quite feverish and joined together in holy matrimony in an emotional state that exceeded the degree of heat from the most intense and potent pepper sauce. But now the honeymoon is long over. The heat has cooled; the urgency of compelling sexual need has been worked out of their system. Over time a repeated pattern has developed: Both go to work every day and come home tired. They eat out or cook something easy, then he loads the dishwasher while she rounds up the dirty clothes and stuffs them in the washing machine. She helps the kids with their homework while he does the work he brought home from the office. After the ten o'clock news, they shower, peck each other on the cheek, and plop into bed. The next day is a rerun of the same, as is the day after and the day after.

Both Eddie and Kristi feel that their life is slipping away. Their appeal will soon fade, and they wonder if there is more to life than they are experiencing. It's a sure setup for a midlife crisis.

So when a good-looking marketing director at a trade convention asks Kristi to dine with him several times and finally suggests further intimacies, she begins to feel that she has missed out on what she really wanted in marriage. This may be her last chance at happiness. Suddenly her vow to Eddie seems a small, distant thing. Surely she has a right to happiness. After all, that's what life is about, isn't it?

REGRET

Now let's look at Eddie. The dullness of his marriage (as he perceives it) leads him to daydream about his high school sweetheart, Megan, the girl he almost married. He remembers how beautiful she was, especially on those moonlit nights in his parked car overlooking the town. He wonders whatever happened to her and decides to look her up on Facebook. *Ah, there she is. Wow! She's still gorgeous!* He invites her to be a Facebook friend. They exchange a number of messages, and he finds out that she is married but unhappy. *Why didn't I marry her when I had the chance?* He begins to regret not marrying Megan, and suddenly his vow to Kristi looms like a boulder blocking his path to real happiness.

Eddie doesn't realize that he has created an illusion. He thinks he is grieving the loss of the woman he didn't marry who could have made him much happier than the one he did. He does not realize that he is idealizing Megan into something she is not and never was. Memory tends to edit the past, elevating the romantic, happy times and submerging the conflicts and the uncertainties. He can't see that if he had married Megan, he would have encountered the same problems as with Kristi, or maybe worse. He regrets not having what he thinks he really wanted, which prevents him from accepting, appreciating, and loving the woman he has.

RISKY CHOICES

When Kristi chose to accept the invitations to dine with the handsome marketing director, she was making a risky choice. She was entering a high danger zone where one false step could cause her to slip and fall. Even worse, she was entering that zone with someone eager to trip her deliberately.

When Eddie connected to his old high school sweetheart on Facebook, he too made a risky choice. It was the perfect setup for an online affair, which often leads to physical affairs. According to a 2009 Loyola University study, "Facebook is cited in one out of every five divorces in the United States."[1]

Suppose Eddie's old sweetheart urges him to attend their high school reunion and meet her face-to-face. Before he responds, he had better think through what might happen in the future if he accepts. In this prerecording of his potential future, he meets Megan and she is bubbly and excited to see him, just as when they were dating. They dance, and she moves closer to him and softens in his arms. He returns home with her much on his mind, and they exchange e-mails and then a few clandestine calls. On a business trip he detours to the town where she lives. They have dinner, and one thing leads to another until she is in his hotel room that night.

The tape of the future continues: After the affair Eddie is even unhappier with his marriage, and he divorces Kristi and marries Megan. The prerecording continues along predictable lines, showing what will happen on down the line. He is marrying a cheater. When the glow wears off their marriage, won't she do it again? Won't he?

It doesn't take an Einstein to know that some situations are risky and should be avoided. That doesn't mean avoiding them later after things start getting out of hand; it means avoiding that first step into the risk zone.

Jim was happily married. At the end of a stressful workday his beautiful young administrative assistant asked him to give her a shoulder rub. Jim did, and as he kneaded her shoulders, she kept moaning, "Oh, that feels soooo good! You really know how to use your hands." The next time it was her shoulders and neck. The next time it was . . . well, you know where things went from there. But the truth is, things were headed there from the beginning.

Frank had successfully resisted porn. But once when his wife was out of town, a salacious e-mail ad popped up on his computer. Curious, he clicked on the icon, which led him to a porn site. He couldn't resist the nude images enticing him there, and he entered the site. From that moment on, he was hooked, and he returned again and again.

Jim and Frank made risky choices and they paid the price. Eddie and Kristi face similar choices. All too often those choices, once made, lead one deeper and deeper into a maelstrom from which people find it almost impossible to extract themselves. Marriage vows are broken, either overtly by seeking divorce or more subtly by violating the promise to love and honor your mate to the exclusion of all others. The only sure way to prevent the downward pull is to resist taking that first, risky step. Once you take it, the other steps become increasingly harder to resist. As Mark Twain said, "It's easier to stay out than get out."

Refusing to plunge into those risky choices before they get a grip on you is a big step toward remaining faithful in your marriage. Every time I refuse to ogle another woman or lust after her I am practicing my vows. Each time I turn the page to avoid a magazine ad featuring a scantily clad model, I am practicing my vows. Every time I honor my wife in a conversation with a friend rather than put her in a negative light, I am practicing my vows. And every time I refuse to click on a website or view a scene in a movie or steer my focus toward another female, I am practicing my vows as an act of commitment to her.

Every time my wife resists the temptation to compare me to another man she is practicing her vows to me. Every time she refuses to read an erotic novel or some unrealistic romance tale, she is practicing her vows to me. Every time she refuses to connect online with someone she dated, she is practicing her vows to me. And every time she refuses to fantasize about someone she sees in a movie or on television, she is practicing her vows to me. In practicing vows in these initial ways, we avoid breaking them in horrific ways.

When a mate does not practice visual, emotional, and social fidelity, the end result is often sexual infidelity.

RULE-BREAKING

Marriage psychologist Dr. Willard F. Harley lists four basic rules designed to help couples fulfill their marriage vows. These rules, which we will explore more fully in a moment, include commitments to each other in the areas of care, protection, honesty, and time.[2]

When Eddie and Kristi stood at the altar and repeated their wedding vows, rules didn't even enter their minds. They gladly made those vows because they were so madly in love that remaining faithful and true was going to be a slam dunk. But a few years into the marriage, the need for those vows became apparent. That hidden, ugly foot appeared. Reality settled in, unsuspected traits emerged, disagreements arose, and the drone of humdrum routine dulled their romance. They found that they didn't always feel like doing the right thing. They felt the urge to do what they wanted instead of what they ought—the urge to follow their feelings rather than to exercise self-discipline and selfless giving.

IF WE ALWAYS FELT LIKE DOING THE RIGHT
THING, WE WOULDN'T NEED LAWS.

That's why we have laws and rules. They prod us to do the right thing even when we don't feel like it. If we always felt like doing the right thing, we wouldn't need laws. Wedding vows are crucial because in the presence of witnesses the couple makes a solemn promise to stick to the rules even when they feel the powerful pull of their wants and urges. Rules remind us to do what love should make us want to do.

The Romance of the Rules

In order to start practicing their lifetime vows, Eddie and Kristi need to do two things. First, they need to spark up and rejuvenate their marriage. When you read that sentence, you probably start thinking of things like more dates, more surprises, more romance, more variety in sex. These changes are all worth considering, but it may surprise you to know that you can spark up your marriage simply by following Dr. Harley's four rules mentioned above—care, protection, honesty, and time.

CARE

Commit to the rule of care and you commit to meeting each other's needs—emotionally, sexually, spiritually, and physically. It means expressing your love and showing your affection. This includes touches, kisses, hugs, cards, gifts, and courtesies. Care means being the other's companion, both in building a life together and in recreational activities. It means being your mate's conversational companion, building intimacy by communicating freely with each other. It may be the most difficult thing you do, but sitting and listening is the communication vehicle of caring. Words still need to be expressed, but sometimes a listening ear is the strongest expression of care.

PROTECTION

Primarily, I view the rule of protection as a function the husband provides for his wife. That means providing a secure home and a safe environment for her and the family. It means accompanying your wife in dangerous areas and defending her against threats of harm. But there are many ways in which both husbands and wives should protect each other. They should protect each other's time, reputation, health, shared secrets, and privacy.

HONESTY

The rule of honesty means being open and transparent with each other. It means holding nothing back, expressing your true feelings, longings, hopes, failures, and needs. The way to intimacy is opening up your hearts to each other and giving your mate full access to who you are.

TIME

The rule of time is something that both partners must honor. Time must be planned, not stumbled upon. Time must be a priority, not a luxury. It needs to include time for eyeball-to-eyeball contact. It needs to include listening and sharing and resolving. It must be consistent and dedicated solely to each other. Young children, needy parents, fantastic friends, or an amazing hobby must never be allowed to eliminate your time together. [3]

Now you can see what I mean when I say that following rules can rejuvenate your marriage. Built into these rules are the very rejuvenating factors every marriage thrives on. While the idea of following rules doesn't seem very loving or romantic, the truth is that the rules keep love and romance rolling by putting us on the track when our lethargy or wandering feelings lure us to go astray. Following these rules makes your wedding vows much easier to keep.

From a Party to a Project

The second thing that would help Eddie and Kristi commit to keeping their vows is to change their view of what marriage is really about. If they can do this, they will find that their marriage is not quite as bad as they think it is. Part of their problem is that, like so many couples, they plunged into marriage thinking it would be a party instead of a project. If it's a party, you expect nothing but good times, fun, and frolic. But if it's a project, that means it involves discipline, work, and goals to be achieved.

I can guess what you're thinking now: making marriage a project takes out all the joy and turns it into a chore. Not so. In fact, the opposite is true. When you think of marriage as a party and then things start going wrong— an argument breaks out, someone gets sick, a storm comes and everyone has to get out of the pool—the party is ruined. It's over and you have nothing to show for it but the mess to be cleaned up.

But when you think of marriage as a project, when difficulties arise you take them in stride. You know that every worthwhile endeavor has its snags. You work through them, and joy comes when the problem is solved and you move on to the next step. Almost all projects involve times of dull routine. A Carnegie Hall concert by a great pianist requires hours and hours of repetitive practice. It's dull, it's tiring, but the end result is breathtaking, spine-tingling music. The everyday things you do in marriage may seem dull and repetitive, but they are building a life together—an achievement that will give you great joy and satisfaction.

Projects can be exhilarating, but not everything involved in them is fun. For me, writing this book is a project. I began it with excitement and great hopes. As I got into it, there were times when I bogged down or got stuck on what I should write next or how to say it in the best way. At times I deleted what I had written and started over. But in plowing through these obstacles, I find gratification in each completed paragraph, each chapter. The momentary obstacles and the tedious hours of research don't put me off because I'm focused on the goal of getting the book into the hands of people it can help.

That's the kind of change in outlook Eddie and Kristi need. It's not so much a change in the substance of their marriage—the work and routine of keeping things running—but rather a change in attitude toward what they are doing.

What Eddie and Kristi now see as a dull and monotonous trap can be seen as a thing of beauty. A stronger focus on the harmony of the music they are performing together can cause the tedium of doing scales to be caught up in the joy of mutual accomplishment. Such a change can cause them to see their vows as they did when they married—so motivated by love for each other that living up to them will be a slam dunk. Expect nothing but a party and you get nothing but a mess to clean up. Expect to tackle a glorious project, and great joy and satisfaction will come as an unexpected by-product.

The Unhappy Consequence of Broken Vows

Breaking wedding vows never leads to anything good. It's either a broken marriage with all the legal, emotional, financial, spiritual, and family fallout that follows, or it's the grueling ordeal of confession, repentance, forgiveness, and rebuilding the shattered relationship from the ground up.

THE HAPPINESS YOU EXPECT TO FIND IN BREAKING
OUT OF A DULL MARRIAGE AND MARRYING
THE PARTNER OF YOUR DREAMS IS A MYTH.

The happiness you expect to find in breaking out of a dull marriage and marrying the partner of your dreams is a myth. People who break vows are not happier. According to the Institute for American Values, "Two-thirds of unhappily married spouses who stayed married reported that their marriages were happy five years later." Or, to flip the coin, "Unhappily married adults who divorced were no happier than unhappily married adults who stayed married. . . . Even unhappy spouses who had divorced and remarried were no happier on average than those who stayed married."[4]

Breaking your wedding vow reveals the truth about your character. It says you are not a person of integrity; your word cannot be trusted. Without a strong commitment to personal integrity, you cannot be happy with yourself, and if you are unhappy with yourself, you cannot be happy with your spouse. While you don't realize it, your unhappiness is not coming from your mate; it's coming from inside yourself.

The absence of character revealed by broken vows explains why they are likely to be broken again. It only makes sense that second marriages end at the rate of 60 to 67 percent and third marriages at a whopping 70 to 73 percent.[5] What else should you expect from a person who does not honor a vow? Marry a person who cheats on his or her spouse, and you can expect to be cheated on.

Of course you don't expect that to happen in your second marriage. You believe you are the exception. You believe you are so amazing that this person who cheated with you would never cheat on you. Most likely you will discover how wrong you can be.

The Bible is very clear that there are exceptions to the rule of no divorce. If your spouse has abandoned you or committed adultery, you have permission from Jesus to divorce. But even when your marriage hits a major pothole like adultery, abuse, or addiction, it is not imperative that you break it off. You can take either of two distinct directions. One, of course, is to divorce. This is the way most accepted by today's culture. But over and over I find that couples who stay together and work through the issues that led to the infidelity build marriages that are often much stronger than those that have not faced such a major challenge. Though awfully painful, the process builds character, which every happy person must have whether married or not. We all need to start realizing that character is vitally important—even more important than our immediate wants, as did the man in the following true story.

General George C. Marshall, US Army chief of staff during World War II and later secretary of defense and secretary of state, married Elizabeth (Lily) Cole in 1902 when he was a twenty-one-year-old second lieutenant. On their wedding night, she revealed that because of a medical condition she could never have sex. This was not like the story earlier of the woman whose reaction to sex on the honeymoon triggered unresolved issues from earlier sexual abuse from her father. She had not known this would happen, but George Marshall's new wife knew and chose not to reveal it until they were married. Most young men would have felt enormously betrayed by such a revelation, no doubt ending the marriage immediately. But not George Marshall. He had made a vow, and he felt duty bound not only to remain married—but also to fulfill his vow by treating his wife with love and honor.

Throughout their twenty-five-year marriage (she died in 1927), he was never unfaithful to her. According to biographer Ed Cray, "Marshall lavished a hundred little attentions on Lily. . . . He fetched and carried. He planned little surprises. He was solicitous about her health and comfort. . . . He paid her innumerable little compliments. . . . He gave her his unremitting consideration, smoothed the path before his queen and led her by his hand."[6]

This kind of character and integrity seems extraordinary and even beyond comprehension today. But it should be the norm for everyone. To be a person of integrity before God, you must practice your lifetime vows. You do it because you said you would. It may not be easy, but I can assure you that it's the ultimate way to joy.

THINGS TO DO IF YOUR SPOUSE
Is Not Practicing Your Lifetime Vows

- Remember that enabling evil does not honor God, especially when your true motive is fear. Sometimes you have to disturb the peace to make peace.

- See the real issue as connection and ask your spouse if the two of you could get some help to rebuild your connection.

- If your spouse will not respond to your requests, ask a pastor or counselor to help you communicate your desire for change.

- If your spouse won't get help or even see a counselor with you, you may need to separate for a time in order for your spouse to feel the consequences of the betrayal.

- To make things stay as they are only encourages an unfaithful spouse to continue in his or her behavior.

- Get support for yourself as you face the reality of your relationship or the lack of your spouse's dedication to it.

- Be sure your spouse knows that if he or she is contrite and repentant that you will extend grace and forgiveness for the rest of your lives.

14

$\Big[$ START SHOWING $\Big]$
RESPECT NO MATTER WHAT

To watch a short video on this subject, go to
7MinuteMarriageSolution.com/14

One of the most surprising realities I see in marriage today is how frequently spouses endure appalling disrespect from each other. It is not an exaggeration to say that mates often show more respect to strangers than to each other. Many husbands and wives discount each other, they are dismissive, or they openly ridicule each other in public. They go far beyond a mere lack of acceptance to finding ways to overtly put down each other or simply ignore the other. Outside of infidelity, disrespect is the most destructive behavior in any marriage.

This is so prevalent and so devastating that repeatedly respect comes up as the most important thing that needs to be there as a foundation for every marriage. Both men and women in the survey I did cited it as the number-one most important thing. Just about every problem can be boiled down to a lack of respect. Adultery is the ultimate lack of respect for your spouse, the institution of marriage, and for God. You can't respect a person while criticizing, trying to change, nagging, hiding money from, or ignoring your spouse.

When there is strong mutual respect, it supports all the other areas needed for a marriage to grow. If respect is not there, that does not mean your marriage is hopeless. You can find respect and give it to your spouse even after years of disrespectful treatment. Let's start with an example of a guy who understood how to show respect to his wife.

When Stan and Lindsey bought their new SUV, they didn't reckon on it being almost too large for their garage. The new vehicle had to be eased in and backed out with great care. Stan hung a tennis ball from the ceiling that touched the center of the windshield exactly when the vehicle should be stopped. "There's almost no wiggle room front-to-back or side-to-side," he told Lindsey. "That means we must always back out with great care to keep from causing damage."

For two months all went well. But one morning Lindsey overslept, putting an important doctor appointment in jeopardy. In her haste, she thrust the gearshift into reverse and hit the gas pedal. As the car zipped out of the garage she heard a sickening crunch as the right side mirror caught the edge of the door frame and buckled like a bulldozed tree.

Stan and Lindsey had recently joined a small Bible study group, and on Sunday night they were hosting the event in their home for the first time. As the couples sat around chatting, one of the men said, "Stan, at church I noticed the crunched mirror on your new SUV. What happened?"

Lindsey held her breath. She was about to be embarrassed and humiliated in front of her new friends.

"Well," Stan responded, "I guess you could say that both Lindsey and I messed up that mirror. One night when I pulled into the garage after working late, I parked the car a tad too far to the right. I should have backed out and reparked, but I was too tired to bother. So the next morning when Lindsey backed out, naturally the mirror caught on the garage door frame."

Lindsey relaxed. It was all she could do to keep from kissing that wonderful man of hers right there in front of everyone.

Stan's response showed his great respect for his wife. He could have done what many husbands do in similar situations. He could have humiliated her with a dumb blonde joke or a deprecating comment about women drivers. Or he could honestly have pointed out that she had ignored his precautions. But he considered his wife's feelings and spared her the humiliation. That is respect.

Respect is the number-one attribute that couples want more of in their marriage. Nothing contributes more toward feeling love or being loved than respect. It is the mother stream from which rivers of blessings will flow into all areas of a marriage. Build respect and you build your relationship. Destroy respect and you negate most of the other positive attributes you bring into the relationship. I think a great place to start in evaluating your role in the relationship is to ask this simple question: "How much do I respect my spouse?" Then ask the follow-up question: "How often and how deeply do I show it?"

Respect grows out of seeing your mate as a person—a marvel of creation highly valued in God's eyes, yet one who is flawed and struggling with sin and selfishness just as you are. When you learn to see your mate as a marvelous gift of God, you will see him or her as the most precious being in your life, to be valued and cherished above all others. We naturally respect and treat well the things we value. But somehow when it comes to one's spouse, that treatment often deteriorates. We revert to our natural self-centeredness and let our moods, irritations, disappointments, or self-interest dictate our behavior. We fail to demonstrate the love we should have for our mates, and that adds up to disrespect.

Disrespect: A Major Wall-Builder

Disrespect, whether in large things or small, comes in many forms—put-downs, rudeness, failure to praise, ignoring, thoughtlessness, and lack of trust, to name a few. The underlying cause of disrespect that lies beneath these behaviors is *objectification*. When you objectify a person, you see him or her as a thing—something to be used for your benefit. Objectifying people means they can be ignored, mistreated, or swept aside when they are not meeting a need. Husbands objectify wives by using them as objects rather than valuing them as humans. She becomes his means of sexual pleasure, of getting children, or of having his meals prepared. Wives objectify husbands by valuing them primarily as a source of income, a meal ticket, or a means of security or having a family.

In my opening example, Stan had a perfect opportunity to objectify his wife by using her as an object of put-down humor. In my experience, Stan's choice to refrain from embarrassing her is not typical. I hear put-downs of mates at nearly every social gathering I attend: "Harry just can't fix anything. Last week it took him two hours and three trips to Home Depot to repair a little faucet leak. And he ended up calling a plumber anyway." "Melinda messes up every joke she tells—always puts the punch line from one joke at the end of another." "I try to get Phil to exercise, but he just lolls in his La-Z-Boy every night and stares at the TV." "Renee tried to make a casserole last week. None of us could eat it, so I gave to the dog. He wouldn't eat it either." "Yes, we'd love to take a cruise, but with what Bob earns it looks like we'll have to settle for another vacation at his mom's."

A husband or wife who makes such comments may think it's merely a harmless form of the common banter that makes up the ongoing battle of the sexes. But this banter is not harmless; it can leave casualties. Maybe the comment is meant for humor, but the element of put-down is there. While the partner may choose to let it roll off, there's usually enough "dig" involved to cause some degree of inner pain. The willingness of a husband or wife to tease or belittle the other, either in public or private, is a passive-aggressive way of objectifying and discounting your spouse, and it is an obvious symptom of disrespect.

I use a lot of stories and humor in my speaking. I can assure you that if I tell a story about my wife, I have already cleared it with her. And afterward you can be sure we will talk about whether the story accomplished what was intended and how it made her feel. If I don't take those precautions, it is only a matter of time before we will be discussing why we feel distance from each other. The last thing I want to do is make her feel uncomfortable or look bad in the eyes of others. To that end she is never made the butt of my jokes. You cannot treat a spouse that way and expect her to be drawn to you.

One of the most common signs of disrespect is simple rudeness, or a lack of common courtesy. After a long day at the office soothing his boss and coddling clients, at home the husband thinks he should be able to relax and "be himself." Often this means he feels justified in dropping all effort to be kind or mannerly. He plops down in his recliner and flips on the news, brushing away his children as they tug at him for attention. His wife brings him a glass of tea and says cheerily, "How was work today?"

"How can you think I'd want to talk about work right now?" he snarls. "Can't you get these screaming brats out of here so I can have a little peace and quiet before dinner?"

The man is thinking only of himself and failing to value his wife, who is doing nothing more than showing interest in him. Scenes like this occur daily all over the nation. It is nothing short of simple disrespect, and it pushes couples apart.

OFTEN PEOPLE ARE MORE RESPECTFUL TOWARD STRANGERS AND PEOPLE THEY WORK WITH THAN TO THE MOST IMPORTANT PERSON IN THEIR LIFE.

I urge you to take the time to evaluate on a regular basis the way you speak to your husband or wife. Often people are more respectful toward strangers and people they work with than to the most important person in their life. They put on their best face when dealing with others, but they tear down and shatter the person who will be there in their future. The more you build up a spouse, the brighter that future is going to be.

Another way spouses disrespect each other is through thoughtlessness. This shows itself in several ways, among them the common complaint that "He never remembers my birthday or our anniversary." Thoughtlessness also occurs when couples fail to pay compliments. He fails to notice her new dress or the new style of her hair. She fails to compliment him on losing twenty pounds. Kind attentiveness needs to become a style of communicating in every marriage, but it is almost impossible if you are holding a grudge or feeding a justifiable resentment. This is where counseling can greatly benefit the two of you. It assists you in wiping the slate clean so that compliments can flow freely and sincerely from your heart.

Disrespect shows up in our failure to express appreciation. She wanted a space to set up an easel and paint. So he spent many evenings and Saturdays designing and building an additional room onto the house. When he finished, it never occurred to her to offer even a simple "thank you." To reward him with a romantic weekend for just the two of them would have been even better.

Disrespect occurs when husbands and wives fail to show interest in the other's achievements. When the kids left home she took up quilting. She did beautiful work, and when she showed him a completed quilt on which she had spent over a hundred hours, he glanced up momentarily from the TV and muttered, "That's nice, dear."

When he retired he bought a rusted '57 Chevy and spent months restoring it to pristine condition. When he proudly showed his wife the finished product, her only comment was, "You don't plan on keeping that old car in our garage, do you?"

It's a sign of disrespect when couples take for granted the everyday work the other does. She cooks, does laundry, cares for the kids, and cleans the house. If he ever thinks about any of these chores, he takes them for granted as just what wives do. He never expresses appreciation. And it works the other way as well. He works eight hours, fights traffic, keeps the yard mowed and trimmed, makes house and plumbing repairs, and helps clean the dinner dishes. In her mind, that's merely what husbands are supposed to do, so it never occurs to her to thank him for it.

A serious evidence of disrespect is breaching the other's trust. When Marty reached his late forties, he began to experience sexual dysfunction. Frustrated and embarrassed, he promised his wife he would see a physician and implored her not to tell a soul about what he was going through. Fortunately the problem was a hormonal imbalance easily solved. But a week or so later a golfing buddy said he'd heard that Marty was having a "little problem" and offered the name of a doctor.

Mortified, Marty confronted his wife, who confessed that she had told only her closest friend, who promised not to breathe a word to anyone.

Marty realized that word of his very private problem had undoubtedly reached many ears, and his humiliation was deep enough that he considered quitting his job and moving to a distant town. Sharing confidences that should be tightly kept between a husband and wife is a serious example of disrespect.

ANY LACK OF ATTENTION OR FAILURE TO CONSIDER
THE OTHER'S FEELINGS IS A FORM OF DISRESPECT.

Any lack of attention or failure to consider the other's feelings is a form of disrespect. It can show up in many other ways that can easily go unnoticed by the one committing the offense. Among these are shaming, blaming, ignoring, provoking, patronizing, dismissing, and controlling. These failures may seem small and inconsequential, but they deprive marriages of the oil that keeps the wheels turning smoothly. Without mutual respect, couples drift apart, and eventually the marriage can grind to a halt.

In my own desire to show more and more respect to my wife, I did some soul searching and came up with something I had not considered before. I am very time conscious and rarely late to any event or appointment. My wife is not that conscious of time. She is conscious of people—making connections and building relationships. I found myself frequently wanting to move her along to the next thing. Most of the time, the next thing could wait or was not much of a priority. I realized I was using my desire to manage her time as a way to control. I did not see this until I looked below the surface and saw that I really wanted her to abide by my timetable. Essentially I wanted her to show respect to me by complying with my rush. But in so doing I was disrespecting her and the parts of her personality that I still marvel at. Today, respecting her in this area has produced a lot less stress for me as I have turned over *my* agenda and submitted to *our* agenda out of respect for her.

Why We Must Respect Each Other

In his famous discourse "The Weight of Glory" C. S. Lewis points out that humans are not "mere mortals." Men and women are not ordinary creatures; we are eternal beings created in the image of God (Genesis 1:27) and worthy of respect.[1] Though God's image in us has been dimmed and blurred by the fall, it is still there beneath our crust of sin, and we bear the capacity to become creatures of dazzling beauty and glory. So both our origin and our destiny give us a strong basis for respecting each other.

Nowhere should that respect be greater or more diligently expressed than in marriage, where two complementary reflectors of the divine image are bonded in a unique love relationship ordained by God himself. Each partner in a marriage must treat the other as a precious being, dearly loved by God. Your mate is paying you the high compliment of lifetime commitment, and that deserves your deepest love, honor, and respect.

Cement Your Marriage with Respect

If you have problems with any of the disrespectful behaviors I've addressed above, it's no good trying to justify your failures with excuses such as, "That's just the way I am" or "I just don't have the time" or "She understands how I am" or "He's just too sensitive about little things." If, for example, you have slipped into a habit of being critical of your husband or wife, that habit can be broken. And breaking it will do much to bring the two of you closer.

If you habitually forget birthdays, anniversaries, and special days such as Valentine's or Mother's Day, you can take decisive steps to change that habit. Get a calendar. Put reminders in your computer, tablet, or phone. You keep business and dental appointments made weeks or months in advance; so you can certainly work into your schedule a way to remember your mate on special occasions. And remember them in ways they appreciate most. Don't send flowers to a woman who would rather you show respect for how hard she works by cleaning the entire house before she awakes on your anniversary.

You can also show your respect by speaking well of her at all times. Do it in front of people around you in person. Do it on social media too. What a great thing to see something respectful and loving for all the world to see! I remember when Misty posted that she loved being married to me. That was amazing to me. Anyone and everyone can say I love my spouse. But to say you love being married to your spouse takes it to a deeper, more meaningful level. At least it did for me.

Maybe you're not a good handyman. You're all thumbs when working with household tools. Still, when you married you took on the responsibility of keeping the house repaired and its plumbing and appliances working. The house is highly important to a wife. It's the nesting place for her family, and to have it snug, neat, and in working order is a big factor in her sense of security. She may subliminally interpret your failure to attend to broken appliances, leaky roofs, peeling paint, and loose carpet as a lack of love, and certainly as a lack of respect. That doesn't mean you must do all these things yourself, but it's important to be attentive to them—spot the problem quickly and either fix it yourself or promptly call a serviceman. Many repairs are easier for klutzes to make now than in the past, as manufacturers have simplified parts and assembly.

I once read a statement by some male celebrity whose name I've forgotten. He said, "It is impossible for a man to treat a woman too well." I think he's right on the money. The simplest way of treating a woman well is to show respect through common courtesy. This also works for a woman treating a man with common courtesy. I know that many feminists disdain the courteous acts men have traditionally performed for women—opening doors, seating her at the table, giving her your seat at a crowded event, or offering to carry things for her. They assume such acts demean women, as if we arrogant males think females are incapable of fending for themselves.

But my own experience says otherwise. In spite of radical feminism, I find that most women appreciate these acts of courtesy and see them as tokens of respect. They make her feel womanly and cherished. They say to her, "You are highly valued. You are worthy of honor and special treatment." The foremost recipient of this kind of respect should be your wife.

Another simple way of showing respect is punctuality. Jason and Mandy show the flip side of the time and punctuality dilemma I mentioned above. It was their second anniversary, and Jason had made reservations at one of the city's most prestigious restaurants. "I'm home! Are you ready?" he called as he walked in the door.

Immediately Mandy emerged from the bedroom fully dressed, every hair in place, and all makeup applied. He was astounded. Such punctuality was not like her at all. Her failure to be ready usually made them ten to twenty minutes late anywhere they went. Mandy saw Jason's surprise and explained. "It suddenly dawned on me that my consistent lateness showed disrespect of you—of your planning, of your time, and of you as a person. I don't want to do that anymore. From now on I will work to be on time in order to give you the respect you deserve." Mandy made a bold move that produced lasting effects on the couple and on the marriage.

AFFIRMING YOUR MATE'S GOOD POINTS AND
BEING GENEROUS WITH COMPLIMENTS IS
AN EXCELLENT WAY TO SHOW RESPECT.

Affirming your mate's good points and being generous with compliments is an excellent way to show respect. When Mandy came out of that bedroom looking as dazzling as a movie star, it gave Jason a perfect opportunity to say, "Wow! You look great!" It is a simple thing, but no one ever gets tired of hearing that they look good.

Be sure, however, that the compliments go beyond appearance and focus on the heart of who she is inside. The same goes for the wife. Maybe he's all thumbs when it comes to house repairs, but that thumb is green as an Irish spring when it turns to landscaping. She should tell him how much she appreciates all he does to make their yard beautiful. And on Saturday when he comes in after spreading fertilizer, showers, and puts on his suit for a friend's wedding, she would do well to look at him with open admiration and say, "Honey, I love to see you working around the house, but when you dress up, you are the handsomest man in the world." Compliments show respect and breed respect.

Respecting Boundaries

So far I've focused on simple but important things husbands and wives can do to show respect. Before I leave the subject, I want to address one element of respect that can loom large in any marriage: respecting boundaries.

Yes, the two of you have joined your lives together in an intimate bond. And in your lovemaking you have become—as Moses, Christ, and Paul affirm—"one flesh" (Genesis 2:24; Matthew 19:5; 1 Corinthians 6:16). That deep intimacy and mystical oneness is vital to a marriage. But it doesn't mean that when you marry you cease to be two individual beings with certain needs unique to each of you.

Respecting boundaries means recognizing your mate's individuality. It means you willingly observe the existence of certain lines that should not be crossed. For example, mates who observe boundaries will not make decisions alone that will affect the other. She has no right to say, as I've heard wives say to neighbors, "George will be glad to come to your house on Saturday and help you build that patio." Nor does he have the right to invite his boss home for dinner without first consulting her.

Individual decisions like these cross a boundary of respect. When observing boundaries you respect each other's differing opinions and approaches. You seek input and advice before making decisions to ensure that whatever is decided does not intrude into the other's zones of safety or comfort.

Respecting boundaries means recognizing certain zones of privacy. If she has an office and he his own study, the other spouse should respect those spaces as the personally controlled domain of each. That does not mean you are not entitled to know what goes on in those places. Both should have free access to each other's computers and phones as a matter of accountability and sexual integrity.

Despite the fact that married couples make their entire bodies intimately known to each other in lovemaking, most couples feel a need for certain zones of bodily privacy. For example, using the restroom is a boundary that should be respected. And even in sex, the most intimate blending of bodies and spirits, there are boundaries to be respected, as I mentioned in chapter 9. Neither should demand of the other any act or performance that is demeaning or repelling. All acts should be mutually satisfying and bring mutual pleasure.

Both spouses are right to set boundaries against physical, verbal, or sexual abuse, and when both partners willingly observe those boundaries, each is showing love and respect.

Only when you respect each other's freedom, needs, and choices can you give yourselves lovingly to one another and bind yourselves together in the kind of intimate oneness that God intends.

An Experiment

Things may have happened in your marriage that cause you to believe you have no reason to respect your mate. He or she has not respected you or has acted in ways that don't deserve respect. Or maybe you have simply drifted apart, each engaging in separate activities. The marriage bond has become so slack that either of you could easily slip through the loop. As a result, your spouse does not seem like the most precious person in your life. You don't feel his or her value as you did when you first married.

———

WHEN YOU BEGIN TO TREAT THE OTHER
PERSON IN YOUR MARRIAGE WITH RESPECT,
THERE'S A GOOD CHANCE IT WILL INCREASE
YOUR RESPECT FOR HIM OR HER.

———

If any of the above is true of you, let me urge you to try a little experiment. We always treat well the things we value—that's easy to understand. But we don't generally realize that this idea can be inverted to good effect: We will begin to value what we treat well. When you begin to treat the other person in your marriage with respect, there's a good chance it will increase your respect for him or her. By treating your mate with respect due to being created in the image of God, you will begin to see the same value God sees in that person. Another good result of showing respect is that in most cases, your mate will respond by showing more respect to you.

I realize how simplistic this may seem. Many marriages that are troubled or going flat have deeper issues that should be addressed and resolved. But if you cannot find a way to respect the person you are with, those other areas will remain as major issues for the marriage. Applying the oil of respect could do much to smooth out the everyday workings of the relationship, thus making the resolutions easier to work out and more likely to succeed.

And if you already have a good marriage, honing your respect can make it even better.

7

THINGS TO DO IF YOUR SPOUSE
Does Not Show Respect to You

- Be sure you are not critical or disrespectful to your spouse.
- Tell your spouse you feel disrespected and ask if there is any unresolved issue that causes your spouse to disrespect you.
- Help your spouse know things to do to show you respect.
- Try to have conversations that search out the feelings behind disrespectful actions to the opposite sex.
- Whenever possible show your respect for the things that are respectful about your spouse. Point out and focus on any positive change your spouse makes.
- Be sure that your spouse knows that getting help together would give you a feeling of priority and respect.
- Continue to explore new ways of raising respect such as involvement in new and interesting projects and hobbies.

PART 3

MINUTES THAT MATTER MOST

THE THREE-STRANDED
CORD OF MARRIAGE

To watch a short video on this subject, go to
7MinuteMarriageSolution.com/15

A strong marriage does not involve only two people. It may surprise you to learn that it was never meant to.

From the beginning, marriage between man and woman was designed to include a third partner. Bear with me as I explain. In Genesis 2:7 the creation narrative hones in on the details of humanity's creation. Here we are told that "God formed a man from the dust of the ground and breathed into his nostrils the breath of life, and the man became a living being" NIV. According to Old Testament scholar Dr. Harold Stigers, this was God's "impartation of the spiritual nature by which he was able to comprehend morality and enabled to enter into fellowship with God."[1] God breathed his own Holy Spirit into the man and his wife.

FROM THE BEGINNING, MARRIAGE
BETWEEN MAN AND WOMAN WAS DESIGNED
TO INCLUDE A THIRD PARTNER.

In Ecclesiastes 4:12, King Solomon compares marriage to a three-corded rope: "A person standing alone can be attacked and defeated, but two can stand back-to-back and conquer. Three are even better, for a triple-braided cord is not easily broken." When you twist three fibers to form a cord, you get more strength in a given length of cord because the twist tightens the fibers into coils to increase the amount of fiber per linear inch. A two-corded rope will unravel quicker than a three-corded rope, because it doesn't have the twisting of the additional cord to increase its strength.

By placing himself in the lives of the man and woman, God completed the rope by becoming the third cord of the marriage. From the beginning marriage was to be a bond of three—man, woman, and God—which made marriage a reflection of the Trinitarian nature of God. God as the third cord gave marriage the strength of three—the strength it needed to withstand the storms that would assail it and to accomplish what God intended man and woman to accomplish.

What were the husband and wife intended to accomplish? This is explained in Genesis 1:28: "God blessed them and said to them, 'Be fruitful and increase in number; fill the earth and subdue it. Rule over the fish in the sea and the birds in the sky and over every living creature that moves on the ground'" NIV. Man and woman were to rule the earth and everything in it as God's deputies. They were to achieve God's plan for populating the globe by producing children who would also carry his image.

Having God as the third cord of the marriage rope completed the joy of the man and woman. They were intimate with God, close to him, in love with him. They loved him as they loved each other, and they found great joy in him. They took daily walks with God.

We know that from that point the story of marriage took a sad turn. Adam and Eve rebelled against God, deciding to go it alone. They thought the two of them could handle things very well on their own, thank you very much. Therefore they excluded God as the third cord of their marriage.

That is why so many marriages are in trouble today. Their marriage only has two cords—husband and wife. They don't have God as the third cord in the marriage to give them the power they need to withstand any storm, any temptation, any attack.

The problem is compounded by the fact that the absence of God leaves an empty place in the marriage—a vacuum that craves to be filled. Like a three-legged stool with one leg missing, it must be propped up with some other substitute to keep it from toppling. When husbands and wives face their brokenness, they sense that something is missing from their marriage. That's when they start seeking something to fill the emptiness—some other third cord that can give them what they are failing to find in their relationship. That is when they often turn to sexual connections outside the marriage, erotic literature, pornography, and various addictive behaviors and substances.

When couples choose one of these progressive problems as the third cord, the trouble intensifies. They go from having a problem to the problem having them. Like a weakened two-cord rope, they become entangled and frayed and too-soon broken. God as the third cord enables them to withstand any attack. But when they turn to something else instead, the thing they turn to becomes the attack itself.

God in his love and mercy is always ready to come back into the marriage and be that third cord as he originally intended. Man and woman once forced him out, so he won't force himself back in. He dearly wants to come in and restore the love, but he must be invited. The problem is that too many couples don't realize God is the missing cord. That is why they turn to substitutes such as porn, eating, spending, gambling, working, or even religiosity.

It is imperative that every couple resist and reject our culture's commonly accepted destructive options that presume to make up that third cord. If any of them have already penetrated your marriage bond, they need to be ripped out before your marriage unravels.

Restoring the Third Cord

When I write of restoring God as the third cord in your marriage, I do not mean just going to church to get your God-card punched, then stuffing your Christianity into your back pocket until the next Sunday. This is the way many Christians live now, but God warned against this through his prophet

Isaiah: "These people come near to me with their mouth and honor me with their lips, but their hearts are far from me" (29:13 NIV).

To strengthen your marriage with God as the third cord, you must reconnect with him the way Adam and Eve connected with him in Eden. You need to walk daily with him in the garden. You must welcome him into your lives as a permanent partner in the marriage. You must get close to him as you do with your husband or wife—and get to know him and his ways so you can begin to see life from his perspective and apply his wisdom to your marriage.

I realize that if you dream of exclusive intimacy between just the two of you, this idea of God as the third party in your marriage may not seem too appealing. Don't marriage triangles cause divorces?

Not when the third corner of the triangle is God. To get my point, draw an equilateral triangle on a sheet of paper. Put your name at the lower right corner of the triangle and your mate's name at the lower left. Then put God's name at the apex—the top of the triangle. Notice that you, your mate, and God are all at the greatest distance from each other. But if you move up your side of the triangle toward God, and your mate moves up the other side of the triangle toward God, you grow closer to each other as you draw closer to God.

Of course, you might think the two of you can just move laterally across the base of the triangle, getting close to each other without having to make the upward ascent. But if you do this you lose your connection with God and fall back to the weakened connection of only two. The only way to get close to each other and yet strengthen your marriage with the power of three is to move up the lines of the triangle toward God.

How to Draw Near to God

How does a couple go about drawing near to God? The way to draw near to your mate is to love him or her. You draw near to God by loving him. Here is where you may encounter a difficulty. Your mate is physically with you, and you can converse, touch, hug, laugh, weep, and do things together. How can you love God as you love your mate when he's not present in a body you can see and touch and hear?

I hope in this book you have already learned that loving your mate means more than just experiencing his or her presence with your five senses—more than having warm feelings and romantic palpitations. These are fine things, and I encourage them. But truly loving each other means so much more. It means getting to know each other intimately, putting the other first, sacrificing for each other, serving each other, giving to each other, respecting each other, accepting each other, and doing things for each other.

WHEN YOU INVEST YOUR LIFE IN GOD,
YOU LOVE HIM ALL THE MORE.

Loving God works in much the same way. It means getting to know him, serving him, respecting him, putting him first, sacrificing for him, giving to him, and doing things for him. When you invest your life in your mate, you love him or her all the more. When you invest your life in God, you love him all the more.

"But," you may ask, "how can I invest my life in both God and my mate? Aren't we warned that we cannot serve two masters?" The answer is that in being husband and wife, the two of you have become one flesh. As one flesh, you act as one in investing your life in serving God. You make it a mutual goal of your marriage to act as one in serving him—your one master—together.

Jesus himself tells us how to love God: "If you love me, keep my commands" (John 14:15 NIV). God's commands are expressions of his love. I know that most people don't think of his commandments in this way. They see them as restrictions on what they want to do. But the truth is, God's commands are meant for our happiness. They tell us how to order our lives to achieve the greatest efficiency, health, love, and joy. He knows, because he created humans, and only he understands what makes us work without ruining us.

Have you ever bought a piece of furniture, an appliance, or some device that had to be assembled? The instructions looked so complex that you decided you could save time and trouble by putting the device together without them. How far did you get before you were ready to kick the thing across the room and call down brimstone on the manufacturer? But when you calmed down and came to your senses, you pulled out the instructions and started over, reading them carefully and following them step-by-step.

I'm sure you're ahead of me and already see the analogy. The only way you can have a satisfying and joyful life is to keep God's commands, and you cannot keep them unless you learn them. That means spending time in the Bible and diligently applying its principles to your lives so you can build your marriage in the way that God designed marriage to be constructed.

To that end, you as a couple need to read some part of the Bible together every day. Even if it is no more than one or two verses, God's word and wisdom will flow from each reading and provide you with new perspectives on God and each other, as well as giving guidance and principles for the conflicts and challenges you face. When you follow those principles, the two of you will draw closer to God. You will be weaving the third cord of the rope solidly into your marriage.

A second way to strengthen the third cord with deeper connection to God is through prayer. I strongly urge the two of you as a couple to pray together every day.

Prayer is one of God's most amazing gifts. Can you imagine being able to pick up the phone and talk to the governor of your state or the president of the United States any time you want? And always with the assurance that whatever he is doing, he will take the call? That is the promise of prayer. We can at any time speak directly, not just to the governor or the president, but to the Creator and Master of the entire universe. And he promises to listen and respond.

You don't have to worry about preparing your prayer as carefully as you would a call to the governor. No doubt you've heard prayers in church composed of eloquent and beautifully intoned phrases. Forget that. Yours does not have to be a big shot–sounding prayer; it does not even have to be original. If you have heard or read a prayer that expresses your feelings, don't hesitate to use it. You can also use the Lord's Prayer that Jesus taught to his disciples in Matthew 6.

I have sometimes heard people complain about using "canned" prayers—prayers that people have copied or have a habit of praying over and over. But sometimes these prayers may be highly useful. There will be times when you don't feel like praying. You are tired. You are down. Your mind is in a whirl, and you don't feel that you are connecting to God or you can't find the words you want. When this happens, you need to pray anyway. That's when a canned prayer can help. It gives you a prayer to pray when you don't feel anything inside you to pray with.

Don't worry about whether your weak, confused, or canned prayers are reaching God. They are, because we have supernatural help. The apostle Paul tells us, "the Spirit helps us in our weakness. We do not know what we ought to pray for, but the Spirit himself intercedes for us through wordless groans" (Romans 8:26 NIV). Just pray the best you can and let the Holy Spirit carry your prayer to the throne of God.

Reading Scripture and praying together can refocus your marriage and build spiritual strength that cannot be achieved in any other way. I strongly recommend that couples spend a minimum of seven minutes together in prayer and Scripture reading every day. I will have more to say about that crucial seven minutes in the next chapter.

Getting into the Word together and being diligent in prayer together are daily essentials to binding that third cord of God into your marriage. Those two actions will draw you nearer to God and increase both your connection to him and your love for him. Having God as the third cord will make your marriage stronger than any external attack Satan can mount against it.

THE MOST IMPORTANT
THING OF ALL

To watch a short video on this subject, go to
7MinuteMarriageSolution.com/16

In this book, you have learned the seven most harmful behaviors to stop and the seven most helpful behaviors to start in your marriage. But in this final chapter I will reveal the most important thing you can do for your marriage. This is the big one. This is the one that clears the path for all the other solutions for a satisfying marriage offered in this book. It will facilitate stopping those negative things that have become so destructive and ease the implementation of the positive things that will transform your marriage and build it up. I have placed this essential part of the 7 + 7 + 7 plan here at the end because I don't want you to forget it. If you and your spouse commit to this simple, seven-minute solution, the best is yet to come.

Maintain the Garden of Your Marriage

Cleaning out the negative stuff from your marriage is only half the battle. You must then add positive attributes to replace what you have torn out, or everything will revert back to the previous stage and deteriorate even further.

A mutually satisfying, long-term marriage, however, requires this crucial, final step past simply replacing the bad stuff with good. Marriage is like a growing garden. To keep it alive and thriving requires continual maintenance and tender care of the delicate and growing plants you place within it.

Stopping the seven things you need to stop is preparing the soil by plowing the hard ground that makes marriages tough. And that ground needs to be plowed over and over again.

Once the hard ground is cleared and plowed, you can set out healthy, flowering plants—the seven things to start doing. But if you clear your land and set out your plants and then walk away, saying, "We've done our job; now we'll just wait for the flowers," you will never see a bloom. The seven things to stop are like weeds and briars that keep trying to creep back in. Unless you are diligent to prevent them, they will take over like a hopeless tangle of weeds, brush, brambles, insects, and raiding varmints returning to create a worse mess than before your plot was cleaned and plowed.

To maintain the seven positive things you have planted in your marriage, you have to cultivate and fertilize the ground continually—irrigate, hoe out the weeds, poison the insects, and fence out the varmints, because those seven things to start are like delicate, tender plants that need to be nourished and protected if they are to grow. Constant diligence is required, or your marriage garden will never produce beauty.

I have a maintenance problem like this in my home office for writing and broadcasting. I'm very good at *getting* organized, but I'm terrible at *staying* organized. When I organize my office, I have a place for everything and everything in its place. I have neatly ordered files, labels, shelves, cubbyholes, and drawers where all my books, papers, manuscripts, writing equipment, research, notes, and correspondence are carefully arranged and stored away. But two months later my office looks like it could qualify for federal disaster aid. My wife won't enter it without updating her tetanus shot. I can barely see over the chaotic jumble strewn across my desk, piled on the floor, stacked haphazardly against walls, and stuffed randomly in shelves. Sadly I lack ongoing diligence to maintain order.

The same thing can happen to your marriage if you fail in your ongoing diligence to maintain the new good you have created. That is why in the previous chapter I urged you as a couple to engage in daily prayer and Bible reading. Those activities draw God into your marriage, giving it order and protection through the unassailable strength of the third cord. Reading and praying are the primary activities that reconnect your marriage with God and draw him back in as your third partner.

The Most Important Thing You Can Do

You must not look on prayer and Bible reading as merely another item on a list of things to do. They are much, much more than that. Spending daily time with God is the most crucial activity the two of you can engage in together. It maintains your marriage, protecting the positives and keeping out the negatives you ripped away in the first fourteen chapters of this book.

Time with God is so important that the apostle Paul says it can even replace sex at intervals in your marriage: "Do not deprive each other of sexual relations, unless you both agree to refrain from sexual intimacy for a limited time so you can give yourselves more completely to prayer. Afterward, you should come together again so that Satan won't be able to tempt you because of your lack of self-control" (1 Corinthians 7:5).

THAT THIRD CORD WILL NEVER BE STRONG
ENOUGH TO KEEP YOUR MARRIAGE ON TRACK
UNLESS YOU BIND YOURSELVES TO GOD DAILY.

That third cord will never be strong enough to keep your marriage on track unless you bind yourselves to God daily. This means spending time together with him every day. Reading to discover the wisdom and insights in God's Word and praying to connect with him must become a habit in your life—something you do as regularly as eating your daily meals. Just as regular meals are essential to the nourishment of your body, regular time with God is essential to the nourishment of your spirit.

You cannot let this time with God drop by the wayside, because it is your key to maintaining what you have cleaned out and replanted in your marriage. These crucial seven minutes of the day build and strengthen the three-cord rope that binds everything else together. All the work you do in the first fourteen chapters of this book is held together by your relationship as a couple with God.

Developing a Daily Devotional Habit

Because of our natural tendency to let distractions interfere with our resolve, I will give you a few pointers for making these seven minutes as powerful as they can be in your life and in your marriage.

DO IT DAILY

Your daily time with God will not just automatically begin and keep going unless you discipline yourselves to make it happen. You and your spouse may start with good intentions, but other cares will quickly interfere. You may miss your time together one day because a child was sick, the plumbing stopped up, you were unexpectedly called away, or your neighbor locked herself out of her house. One of you may be out of town, working overtime, or ill.

Those are all legitimate reasons for missing your devotional time together that day. Even the strict laws of the Old Testament Sabbath allowed exceptions to the no-work rule. They were expected to tend to emergencies—pulling out an ox that had fallen into a ditch, for example. Things will come up now and then. The problem is that when you miss your time with God once, it's that much easier to miss it the next time.

Allow for occasional interruptions. But make an ironclad pact with each other to create the devotional habit and keep it going. The bottom-line goal is to do this more often than not. Based on the Center for Biblical Engagement, no fewer than four days a week is required to produce the results of a strong, lasting, intimate marriage.

KEEP IT SHORT

If you begin your time with God together by allowing the sessions to run too long, it will become difficult to maintain the habit in the future. Twenty or thirty minutes may seem great at first before the newness wears off, but as you continue, other duties will press in and you will be tempted to omit the devotional "just for today" because it takes so much time and your schedule is too crowded.

I recommend seven minutes as the minimum. In seven minutes you have time to read a short devotional, discuss it briefly, read two Scripture passages, and pray together. Seven minutes will not take such a chunk out of your day as to create a time problem, which means you will never have to approach it with dread because you have so many other things to do. If, after you have set your devotional habit firmly, you and your spouse get into a discussion and want to go longer, don't hesitate. Go as long as you like. Or better yet is to continue to discuss your seven minutes together throughout the day. Observe your seven-minute minimum and don't let your devotionals become a time burden for either of you.

KEEP THINGS RELAXED AND COMFORTABLE

The seven-minute devotionals can be set up at any time and in any place where both of you feel relaxed and comfortable. You must take care to be free of television, books, magazines, kids, pets, or any other interruptions.

When I am home, my wife, Misty, and I meet together almost every night just before bedtime. We look at each other eye to eye, listening, sharing and reconnecting after a tough day. It seems that no matter what we have been through or how hard the day, our meeting time brings us back together to reconnect and strengthen our bond with each other and God. Morning can serve you well to focus your day on what really matters. It can be a reminder to incorporate God into every part of your day. It can be an early connection point before the world tries to pry you apart in every way possible.

CONSIDER READING A DAILY DEVOTIONAL BOOK

Find a good source for some kind of daily devotional thought for your time together. It should address a specific challenge or provide insight into a tough issue relevant to your marriage. Bookstores have shelves loaded with any number of books of short daily devotionals. There are many devotionals on marriage written by well-known and reliable authors. Many couples read a devotional each day from books of this sort and find them helpful in giving examples or insight into issues all couples tend to face.

READ FROM THE BIBLE

Devotionals are optional in your seven minutes with God, but Bible reading is not. In every seven-minute session it is vitally important that you read a short passage of Scripture together. Engaging with the Bible daily produces positive change, builds character, and greatly reduces the temptation toward marriage killers such as pornography, gambling, and sex outside of marriage. As I mentioned, the Center for Biblical Engagement research shows that engaging with God's Word at least four times a week is the minimal amount of time required to produce change. The change won't be instant, but I think you will be astounded at the transformation that will occur in you and your spouse as you continue. You will probably notice it first in some little attitude change that doesn't mean much. Then you will see the change crop up when you say no to some temptation or distraction you would not normally pass up. Eventually you and your mate will see each other in a different and better way. You will be living with the power of God's Word in your lives.

To keep your Bible reading meaningful, I recommend thematic readings that will help you focus on scriptures relevant to your relationship with God and each other. Unless you are a Bible scholar, I doubt that you will find much inspiration in reading chapter after chapter explaining the intricate details of the Mosaic Law in Leviticus or the many chapters of genealogies in the book of Numbers. To keep your readings relevant, you need some kind of guide to help you locate appropriate scriptures.

One solution is to use thematic study Bibles. There are many that are organized around specific themes drawn from a wide range of subjects, including marriage. You might find one of these to be a helpful guide in your daily readings.

It is very important that you keep these Bible readings on a mutually beneficial level. Both of you should go into the readings as learners. For this and other reasons, neither of you should assume the role of teacher to the other. If either of you had the Bible crammed down your throat in the past, that negative history can cause resentment when one spouse presumes to teach the other. Remember that you are equal partners walking side-by-side on a journey together. Neither of you is on a leash in the hands of the other. Each of you must always approach Scripture gently and humbly.

Not long ago I counseled a wonderful guy whose wife had just left him. Years earlier he discovered that he had biblical grounds for divorcing her, but he chose to hang in there and try to work it out. One thing that complicated their relationship was something you would think should be a great asset to any marriage. In spite of her wayward ways, she was, of all things, a Bible teacher. At least, she thought of herself as such. In an attempt to keep their marriage intact, they tried to read the Bible together.

But every time they opened the Book, she became the "teacher" and used scriptures to make her case against him and justify her infidelity. (No doubt you have already learned that people with impure motives can find a way to prove anything they want by using selective Bible verses, wrenching them out of context, and discarding commonsense meanings.) This couple's experience is a stark illustration showing the high importance of mutuality in reading God's Word together.

As one way to encourage mutuality in Bible study, I suggest that both you and your mate participate in the reading. Each of you can read separate passages of Scripture.

PRAY TOGETHER

Of equal importance with Bible reading is prayer. As I said in the previous chapter, your prayer need not be fancy or polished. It need not even be original. But I urge you to make it relevant to you and your mate, and let it come from your heart. Don't just pray for what you think you ought to pray for.

When you pray, consider holding each other's hands or making physical contact in some way. It is good for your prayer to involve each other, your relationship, or some desire you share or issue you face. Whatever else you pray for, be sure to ask God to help you to live together with love and grow together in wisdom and character.

When praying, let me suggest that rather than close your eyes, try something that my wife and I find very bonding. Hold each other's hands and look in each other's eyes as you pray for each other. This is simple but so powerful that the effect lasts far beyond the seven minutes. And the more you do it, the more you may find that any defensiveness between the two of you is eradicated. You begin to feel that you are truly on each other's side, pulling for each other to experience the best that God has.

I realize that saying this 7 + 7 + 7 plan will fix your marriage is a grand claim. And for such a claim to be true, you would think it would be something newly discovered or deeply profound. But as I mentioned in the introduction, having a strong marriage is easier than you might think. The truth is, there is no new discovery more profound than the impact of a couple taking a mere seven minutes out of each day to be together with God. The devotional thought expands your perspective. The Word of God, if read at least four times each week, changes behavior and character. Praying together provides a spiritual connection between all three persons in the triple-braid cord.

Before you write off taking these crucial seven minutes of daily couple time with God as too simple to help or too complicated to implement, just try it for thirty days. After a mere month, you will discover significant changes in both of you and new hope for your relationship.

Using the *7 Minute Marriage Solution Devotional Bible*

As I stated earlier, you should feel free to use any devotional resources that best fit you and your needs. Because I feel it is so important for couples to spend time together with God, I have headed up a team that put together a devotional Bible for just that purpose: *The 7 Minute Marriage Solution Devotional Bible*. As you might guess by the title, this devotional Bible was created to be a companion to the book you now hold in your hands.

This Bible contains 260 devotionals placed throughout the biblical text, giving couples a meaningful devotional to share five days per week—Monday through Friday—for an entire year. On weekends I urge you to enjoy biblical teaching, encouragement, and fellowship within your church community.

These devotionals are themed on marriage-related topics such as communication, sexual intimacy, parenting, acceptance, forgiveness, and the like. Alongside each devotional is a poignant quotation relating to some aspect of the devotional and designed to spark discussion. These quotations are gleaned from the writings of respected authors, counselors, and pastors known for their knowledge and wisdom on marriage topics. Two sets of short Scripture passages, one to be read by the husband and one by the wife, accompany each devotional.

In my opinion, among the most valuable elements in these devotionals are the prayer starters at the end of each. These are brief beginning phrases designed to help you continue on with your own words, leading you to pray your own prayers together.

I believe *The 7 Minute Marriage Solution Devotional Bible* will make your seven minutes easy to implement and powerful beyond your expectations. It is specifically designed to accommodate the elements of a couple's devotional I have outlined in this chapter. Use it faithfully, and I am confident God will use it in your transformation process.

The Best Seven Minutes of Your Marriage

Allow me to reemphasize the importance of this seven-minute connection. I am convinced that the daily seven minutes you spend getting closer to God and each other will be the most important—even the most crucial—seven minutes in your marriage. Those seven minutes can build cumulative blessings into your relationship for years to come. They can lead you to the ultimate solution to every marriage problem you have. I don't mean there is anything magical or mystical about the seven minutes or that just going through the ritual of Bible reading and prayer will automatically untie every knot in your marriage. Calling these seven minutes a "solution" to your marriage difficulties does not mean an instant cure.

What it means is this: if you put yourself into these seven minutes and take them seriously as time you are investing in your mate and your God, and if you open your mind as you read the Bible and your heart as you pray, the blessings you receive in return will inspire and enable you to become the kind of selfless, serving, and loving being that makes marriages work. God will give you wisdom from his Word and a connection with him through prayer that will develop in both of you the inner peace and strength needed to accomplish all the other "stops" and "starts" involved in achieving a successful marriage.

Stop the seven most harmful behaviors. Start the seven most helpful ones. Do it all while spending the most important seven minutes of the day together with God, and your marriage will be transformed!

May God bless you as you learn daily to cling to him and to each other.

STUDY GUIDE

---

ere's a chance to apply in your life what you've read in this book. Try the 7 + 7 + 7 plan and watch your struggling marriage find new life or your good marriage get even better!

These questions are designed to discuss with your spouse and also with a group. If you need assistance in starting or facilitating a group, please call 800-NEW-LIFE and ask to speak the director of group support.

As you read these questions, look for what you can learn about yourself rather than what you hope your spouse will notice and respond to.

WEEK 1

Watch Steve's introductory video at 7MinuteMarriageSolution.com/intro

Chapter 1: STOP CLINGING to Unrealistic Expectations

Watch Steve's introductory video at 7MinuteMarriageSolution.com/1

DISCUSS WITH YOUR SPOUSE

- What unrealistic expectations did you bring into the marriage? Or, put differently, what issues had you not thought through or talked through? Consider mutual goals, compatibility on practical matters, values, religion, backgrounds, parentage, economic expectations, children, anger, and so on.

- What are you doing to let go of those unhelpful expectations?

- Read these sentences carefully: "Many perceived flaws in your mate are likely nothing more than unmet expectations on your own part. He may never earn the money to live in the style you hoped for, or she may not have the cooking skills or sexual interest you dreamed of." Acknowledge a specific instance of this, apologize to your spouse, and ask God to help you let go of that toxic expectation—and any others you have.

- What gender differences have caused sparks—or worse? What about those differences can you see being a blessing in some way?

- Now consider differences in family background and upbringing. Each of you name one difference you've had to work through (household chores, holiday celebrations, extended family, and so on) and what has helped.

APPLICATION

Grieve the loss of the fantasy marriage so you can accept the reality of what you have. Seek God to fulfill you and heal you rather than expect your spouse to do what only God can do.

Turn to page 16, and each of you choose one thing to do this week from the "7 Things to Do If Your Spouse Won't Stop Clinging to Unrealistic Expectations."

Chapter 8: START EMBRACING Friendship and Fun

Watch Steve's introductory video at 7MinuteMarriageSolution.com/8

DISCUSS WITH YOUR SPOUSE

- Remind your spouse of a time when laughter defused tension, turned a situation into good, or lifted your spirits. Then switch and let your spouse share an experience of laughter.

- What things give you the chance to laugh with each other? Also, what couple(s) do you both find it easy to laugh and have fun with?

DISCUSS WITH YOUR GROUP

- Friends focus on common things they enjoy. Think back to the early days of your relationship. What did you do then that was fun for both of you?

- What new fun things have you discovered since you got married—or might you try after listening to others in the group?

APPLICATION

Remember two things. First, activity and exertion outside the bedroom often lead to more sexual activity in the bedroom. Second, the couple that plays together stays together.

Turn to page 108, and each of you choose one thing to do this week from the "7 Things to Do If Your Spouse Is Resistant to Having Fun."

WEEK 2

[FOLLOW UP ON LAST WEEK'S 7 THINGS TO DO]

The spouse whose birthday is nearer to your anniversary reports in first.

Chapter 2: STOP OBSESSING on the Past

Watch Steve's introductory video at 7MinuteMarriageSolution.com/2

DISCUSS WITH YOUR SPOUSE

- The most destructive choice you can make in the face of a repentant offender is to hold the past against him or her. Gently tell your spouse what he/she does—if anything—to make you feel as if your past is being held against you. If this isn't an issue, be grateful—and move on to the next question.

- Whether you are obsessing, your past is being obsessed about, or neither, what instruction do you personally hear in Jesus' Golden Rule: "Do to others whatever you would like them to do to you" (Matthew 7:12)? Give a few examples of what treating your spouse the way you would like to be treated would look like today . . . and tomorrow.

DISCUSS WITH YOUR GROUP

- What have you done—and/or what could you do—to become an expert on your mate's hurts? Be specific about the what, not about the hurts.

- In what ways do you extend grace to your spouse when he/she hurts you?

APPLICATION

Trust always involves risk. We must plunge in and trust and love and forgive with no absolute certainty that we will never be hurt again. It is the only way to restore a relationship and the only way to have a strong marriage.

Turn to page 29, and each of you choose one thing to do this week from the "7 Things to Do If Your Spouse Won't Stop Obsessing on Your Past."

Chapter 9: START RESPONDING Romantically to Your Mate

Watch Steve's introductory video at 7MinuteMarriageSolution.com/9

DISCUSS WITH YOUR SPOUSE

- Romance must be a way of life. What can you do to put your spouse first and to show him/her you are aware of his/her needs? You'll find some ideas on pages 115–16, and ask your spouse to identify his/her favorites.

- What can you do to become more able to communicate—or more comfortable communicating—your sexual needs and preferences?

DISCUSS WITH YOUR GROUP

- What one truth about sex do you wish you'd known before you said "I do"?

- Men and women tend to separate romance from sex, whereas the two are meant to intertwine. Brainstorm some ways to interweave romance and sex in a marriage.

APPLICATION

Sexual satisfaction comes from investing in the other person's joy and pleasure. It doesn't come from seeking to gratify yourself. Simply put, the key to satisfying sex is for both of you to learn to expect nothing but to enjoy what is given.

Turn to page 122, and each of you choose one thing to do this week from the "7 Things to Do If You and Your Spouse Are Not Experiencing Sexual Satisfaction."

WEEK 3

[FOLLOW UP ON LAST WEEK'S 7 THINGS TO DO]
The spouse whose birthday is closer to today's date speaks first.

Chapter 3: STOP DROWNING in Suspicion and Jealousy

Watch Steve's introductory video at 7MinuteMarriageSolution.com/3

DISCUSS WITH YOUR SPOUSE

- If trusting your spouse doesn't come easily, what unresolved experience from your past may be fueling it? (See pages 32–33 for a few possibilities.)

- What, if anything, are you doing to cause your spouse not to trust you? (Your spouse may be able to help you identify certain behaviors.) Take responsibility, correct the issue, and do what you need to do to rebuild trust.

DISCUSS WITH YOUR GROUP

- If distrust exists in a marriage, what positive steps can spouses take to uncover the causes and then work on those issues to rebuild trust?

- The best marriages are those in which each spouse builds trust and acts to preserve trust and repair it when it is breached. What acts build trust? What behaviors maintain trust? And what are ways to repair trust when it is breached?

APPLICATION

Your willingness to take firm steps to maintain trust not only speaks volumes, but also makes your mate feel highly valued and protected.

Turn to page 40, and each of you choose one thing to do this week from the "7 Things to Do If Your Spouse Won't Stop Drowning in Suspicion and Jealousy."

Chapter 10: START EXPRESSING Grace and Forgiveness

Watch Steve's introductory video at 7MinuteMarriageSolution.com/10

DISCUSS WITH YOUR SPOUSE

- When you were growing up, what did you learn about accepting responsibility for your wrong and hurtful behaviors? About asking forgiveness? About granting forgiveness? How do those lessons help or hurt your marriage?

- What have you learned in your marriage about the wisdom of Jesus' teaching to put no limits on forgiveness? And what has marriage taught you about the freedom that comes with forgiving as well as with being forgiven?

DISCUSS WITH YOUR GROUP

- To forgive yet allow destructive behavior to continue is called enabling, or codependence. Forgiving means setting boundaries for future behavior and requiring change—and even, in appropriate cases, reparation. Give an example—hypothetical or real-life—of forgiveness and boundaries going hand in hand.

- Why do you think we find it hard to forgive ourselves? What truths and/or practices have helped you forgive yourself?

APPLICATION

Instead of taking offense, choose to forgive your spouse and extend grace to him or her every day.

Turn to page 132, and each of you choose one thing to do this week from the "7 Things to Do If Your Spouse Does Not Express Grace and Forgiveness."

WEEK 4

[FOLLOW UP ON LAST WEEK'S 7 THINGS TO DO]
The spouse whose first name has fewer letters goes first.

Chapter 4: STOP TRYING to Change Your Mate

Watch Steve's introductory video at 7MinuteMarriageSolution.com/4

DISCUSS WITH YOUR SPOUSE

- Consider the things you tend to criticize or nag your spouse about. Be specific as you apologize right now. After both of you have an opportunity to do that, identify any issues (running up the credit card, addiction, etc.) that may actually threaten your marriage.

- You should not set out to change your mate without looking first in the mirror. What change in yourself is at the top of your list?

DISCUSS WITH YOUR GROUP

- Saying "I do" tends to gradually turn slightly irritating or even charming idiosyncrasies into big annoyances. Why do you think that happens? What can we do to stop being annoyed by what once didn't bother us so much?

- What is the value of accepting the fact that some of the things that bother you about your mate will never change? In what ways will you, your spouse, and your relationship benefit?

APPLICATION

Rather than pray for God to change your spouse, pray that God would give you the supernatural ability to be more accepting of your spouse. Acceptance does not change your mate into the tidy or punctual or financially responsible or _____ mate you wish he/she were. But acceptance does change you, enabling you to love your mate in spite of the flaws.

Turn to page 51, and each of you choose one thing to do this week from the "7 Things to Do If Your Spouse Won't Stop Trying to Change You."

Chapter 11: START AFFIRMING Your Mate's Strengths

Watch Steve's introductory video at 7MinuteMarriageSolution.com/11

DISCUSS WITH YOUR SPOUSE

- To receive acceptance and affirmation, you must give acceptance and affirmation. So turn to your spouse right now and list three things you love about his/her personality. Then affirm three of his/her strengths that you appreciate.

- What could your mate do to help you be more comfortable in your own skin without having to worry that you're being continually monitored for acceptability? Be specific—and coach your spouse gently.

DISCUSS WITH YOUR GROUP

- When has someone's acceptance of you given you the freedom to grow, change, or accomplish something? Why does acceptance have that effect on people—including spouses?

- Marital unfaithfulness; physical, mental, or psychological abuse; illegal behaviors or addictions, as to alcohol, drugs, gambling, or pornography—these must not be tolerated. If you find yourself facing one of those issues, you must not accept the behavior, but you must accept the person who separates himself from the behavior. What would you require that separation from the behavior to entail?

APPLICATION

When you travel toward acceptance and affirmation, you flee from the impossible ideal and into the real. You identify and appreciate your spouse's good qualities. Then, just as God in his grace covers our sins with his love, you have the privilege of covering the sins and flaws of your mate with your own love. Marriage is an opportunity God gives us to reflect the nature of Christ and to love as he does.

Turn to page 139, and each of you choose one thing to do this week from the "7 Things to Do If Your Spouse Does Not Affirm Your Strengths."

WEEK 5

[FOLLOW UP ON LAST WEEK'S 7 THINGS TO DO]
The spouse who has lived more places reports in first.

Chapter 5: STOP SEETHING in Anger and Resentment

Watch Steve's introductory video at 7MinuteMarriageSolution.com/5

DISCUSS WITH YOUR SPOUSE

- There are right ways and wrong ways to deal with anger. What did you learn about anger growing up? Was it good/bad, acceptable/forbidden? What did you see and therefore learn about how to handle anger?

- Consider two spiritual aspects of anger. First, most anger is rooted in self-centeredness, so logically the antidote to anger is humility. Second, good counsel for dealing with anger is "Act better than you feel"—and self-control, one of the fruits of the Spirit, enables us to act on that counsel. What apology, if any, does either of these statements prompt you to make to your spouse? Do so! What new or renewed effort will you make in response to one of these truths? If time allows, pray together right now about the issue of anger in your marriage.

DISCUSS WITH YOUR GROUP

- What was your initial reaction to the statement (below)? Do you agree? Why or why not? Are there any exceptions? What did these sentences help you see about yourself?

  > Most of your anger is self-centered. You get angry because you want the world around you to be ordered in a certain way, and when you can't have it that way, you do what an undisciplined child does: you throw a tantrum, pout, or start planning revenge. It's all about you, your entitlement, and what you want right now.

- Listen; repeat your mate's points; offer a rebuttal—this is the common approach to conflict resolution. What have you learned through the years about how to deal with anger, irritation, passive-aggressive behavior, the silent treatment, rage, and conflict? Share some ideas with the group.

APPLICATION

Take to heart Ephesians 4:31–32: "Get rid of all bitterness, rage, anger, harsh words and slander, as well as all types of evil behavior. Instead be kind to each other, tenderhearted, forgiving one another, just as God through Christ has forgiven you." Consider memorizing this passage together with your spouse.

Turn to page 67, and each of you choose one thing to do this week from the "7 Things to Do If Your Spouse Won't Stop Seething in Anger and Resentment."

Chapter 12: START SPENDING Money Responsibly

Watch Steve's introductory video at 7MinuteMarriageSolution.com/12

DISCUSS WITH YOUR SPOUSE

- Turn to page 142. Take a deep breath, say a silent prayer, and then together identify any tough choices you need to make, tough habits you need to break, false assumptions you need to give up, certain actions you need to surrender, or certain steps you need to take.

- If financial conflict is a reality for you and your spouse, try to identify some of the reasons for overspending (insecurity; the rush of freedom; be like your peers; hurt or resentment of spouse, etc.).

DISCUSS WITH YOUR GROUP

- This chapter addresses separate banking accounts, budgeting, credit-card debt, and savings. What insight or tip from this chapter did you find especially helpful?

- Why is it significant that everything in this universe belongs to God, including your money? What does that truth imply about the responsibility of spending and managing money? What are some of the benefits of tithing?

APPLICATION

Most couples face financial difficulty because they do little or no planning or exercise little or no discipline regarding the use of their money. Clarity in the area of finances, however, can lead you and your spouse to security and satisfaction that will benefit you for years to come.

Turn to page 154, and each of you choose one thing to do this week from the "7 Things to Do If Your Spouse Doesn't Spend Money Responsibly."

WEEK 6

[FOLLOW UP ON LAST WEEK'S 7 THINGS TO DO]

The spouse who knows more about current events goes first.

Chapter 6: STOP TOLERATING Compulsions and Addictions

Watch Steve's introductory video at 7MinuteMarriageSolution.com/6

DISCUSS WITH YOUR SPOUSE

- Talk about the difference between peacekeeper and peacemaker. Talk about the difference between hurt and harm. Then explain why you agree or disagree with this statement: "Inflicting pain on a spouse in order to address a harmful behavior can be a lifesaver for the marriage."

- "Better than" morality exists across the board, not only in the areas of compulsions and addictions. Why is this thinking fallacious? And be honest with yourself if not with your spouse as well: where are you guilty of "better than" morality to justify your sin?

DISCUSS WITH YOUR GROUP

- Think about people you know. What has kept/is keeping a friend in an unhealthy, dysfunctional, even dangerous relationship? Why do people in such situations often not hear their friends' concerns about the spouse's drinking, drug use, unfaithfulness, sexual addiction, or gambling?

- As someone has said, "Don't expect functional behavior from a dysfunctional person." That's one reason why the only reliable way to address an addiction is through outside professional help. Why do people hesitate to get professional help? What are some good places to go for help—or to start looking?

APPLICATION

If you are dealing with a compulsion or an addiction, take firm steps of repentance and reform under the power of God's Spirit. If your spouse is dealing with a compulsion or an addiction, look at him or her through God's eyes, remind yourself that the sin is only one part of who your mate is, and then forgive as you want to be forgiven.

Turn to page 82, and each of you choose one thing to do this week from the "7 Things to Do If Your Spouse Is Tolerating Your Compulsion or Addiction."

Chapter 13: START PRACTICING Your Lifetime Vows

Watch Steve's introductory video at 7MinuteMarriageSolution.com/13

DISCUSS WITH YOUR SPOUSE

- Most broken marriage vows are the result of selfishness. What can you do to stand against these four categories of selfishness: routine, regret, rule-breaking, and risky choices? Review the discussion on pages 157–61.

- Marriage psychologist Dr. Willard F. Harley lists four basic areas of commitment designed to help couples fulfill their marriage vows and spark up their marriage: care, protection, honesty, and time. Why is each one of those areas of promise key to a lasting marriage? Along those same lines, what can you do to practice your vows? To get started, review the "Every time . . ." paragraphs for a husband and a wife on pages 160–61.

DISCUSS WITH YOUR GROUP

- God looks upon a vow as an extremely serious thing; we as a culture don't. Any inconvenience, any conflict, any problem, any loss of attractiveness or romantic feeling, or any appealing man or woman on the other side of the fence can often cause one partner to renege on the vow and break up the marriage. What can we as a culture, what can we as a church, what can each of us as a spouse do to strengthen or—perhaps more accurately—recover this respect for vows?

- Focusing on the last sentence, comment on this analysis of why marriages fail. Do you agree or disagree? And if you agree, what can be done about "unhappiness . . . coming from inside yourself"?

Breaking your wedding vow reveals the truth about your character. It says you are not a person of integrity; your word cannot be trusted. Without a strong commitment to personal integrity, you cannot be happy with yourself, and if you are unhappy with yourself, you cannot be happy with your spouse. While you don't realize it, your unhappiness is not coming from your mate; it's coming from inside yourself.

APPLICATION

As Mark Twain said, "It's easier to stay out than get out." Refusing to plunge into those risky choices before they get a grip on you is a big step toward remaining faithful in your marriage. Bottom line, to be person of integrity before God, you must practice your lifetime vows. You do it because you said you would.

Turn to page 167, and each of you choose one thing to do this week from the "7 Things to Do If Your Spouse Is Not Practicing Your Lifetime Vows."

WEEK 7

[FOLLOW UP ON LAST WEEK'S 7 THINGS TO DO]
The spouse who has an easier time walking away from chocolate reports in first.

Chapter 7: STOP FOCUSING Only on Your Interests

Watch Steve's introductory video at 7MinuteMarriageSolution.com/7

DISCUSS WITH YOUR SPOUSE

- To what current issue in your life can you apply the guideline below? If nothing comes to mind, discuss the guideline's value and perhaps even a time in the past when it would have been helpful.

   In a mature relationship where love for the other prevails over self-interest, the question becomes not who wins or who is right, but rather *what* is right. What is best for my husband or my wife? For our marriage?

- Harmonious marriage requires self-interest to be subjected to or at least balanced with the happiness and well-being of the other. What little things can you do to improve your mate's life or make your mate's day better? What comforts or attentions does your spouse value that you could supply? Be creative!

- In what areas of life have you struggled most for self-interest to give way to "we interests"? What areas of selfishness has marriage been forcing out of you? Why does empathy help us self-centered human beings to die to self?

- What concept for marriage did you find new and/or helpful in this chapter's discussion of the following?

Submission   Surrender   Headship

The analogy of pairs skating (pages 86–88)

APPLICATION

Submission of the wife says the same thing to her husband that the female skater says to her male partner: "I trust you. I have faith in you. You will support and protect me if I put myself in your hands." Submission of the husband says the same thing to his wife that the male skating partner says to the female: "You are vital to this partnership. I honor you and support you fully as the center of all we work to accomplish together." Mutual submission binds you together.

Turn to page 93, and each of you choose one thing to do this week from the "7 Things to Do If Your Spouse Won't Stop Focusing Only on Self-Interest."

Chapter 14: START SHOWING Respect No Matter What

Watch Steve's introductory video at 7MinuteMarriageSolution.com/14

DISCUSS WITH YOUR SPOUSE

- Look in the mirror—not your spouse's mirror. What disrespectful words and ways do you need to apologize for and stop? Rudeness, thoughtlessness, ridicule, lack of appreciation, lack of interest in your spouse's achievements, taking for granted his/her everyday work, breaching your spouse's trust, failing to consider his/her feelings, shaming, blaming, ignoring, provoking, patronizing, dismissing, nagging, criticizing, and controlling have no place in a healthy marriage.

- On a more positive note, which of the following will you add to your repertoire this week? You might ask your spouse which two or three would mean the most: being courteous, speaking well of your spouse at all times, keeping confidences confidential, getting a calendar for birthday and anniversary, being punctual, affirming your mate's good points, being generous with compliments about the internal as well as the external, honoring boundaries, and respecting his/her differing opinions and approaches. Right now sincerely affirm a couple of your mate's good points and express gratitude for his/her everyday work.

DISCUSS WITH YOUR GROUP

- Share a time when your spouse's expression of respect had you standing tall, feeling overwhelmed with gratitude, and/or falling more in love. And consider the converse: Why is disrespect in a marriage so destructive?

- An underlying cause of disrespect is objectification. When we objectify a person, we see him or her as an object—something to be used for our benefit, something that can be ignored, mistreated, or swept aside when they are not meeting a need. What can we do to see our mate as a marvelous gift of God, as the most precious being in your life, to be valued and cherished above all others? We naturally respect and treat well the things we value.

APPLICATION

We always treat well the things we value, and we will begin to value what we treat well. When you begin to treat your spouse with the respect due a being created in the image of God, there's a good chance it will increase your respect for him or her. And in most cases your mate will respond by showing more respect to you.

What positive step will you take in response to today's discussion? Some options are listed in the "7 Things to Do If Your Spouse Does Not Show Respect to You" on page 181.

WEEK 8

[FOLLOW UP ON LAST WEEK'S 7 THINGS TO DO]
The spouse who, in the course of this study, has started these follow-ups fewer times goes first.

Chapter 15: The Three-Stranded Cord of Marriage

Watch Steve's introductory video at 7MinuteMarriageSolution.com/15

DISCUSS WITH YOUR SPOUSE

- From the beginning marriage was to be a bond of three—man, woman, and God. As the third cord, God gives marriage the strength to withstand any storm, any temptation, any attack. When did you first hear about God being the third strand in a marriage? If this is the first time, what about the design makes sense or sounds especially valuable? Evaluate together how strong that third cord is or isn't in your marriage—and why.

- You draw near to God by loving him—by getting to know him, serving him, respecting him, putting him first, sacrificing for him, giving to him, and doing things for him. When you invest your life in God, you love him all the more. What is each of you doing to get to know God better? to serve him? What evidence in your individual life and in your life as a couple shows that you are putting God first? What do your answers suggest to you about a course of action?

DISCUSS WITH YOUR GROUP

- To strengthen your marriage by having God as the third cord, you need to spend time with him daily. One practical way of doing this is by obeying God's commands, which you learn by reading the Bible. Share with the group approaches to Bible study or Bible study guides that have worked for you as a married couple.

- A second way a couple spends time with God is by praying together. Share with the group approaches to prayer that have worked for you as a couple.

APPLICATION

- Talk about a time when you were very aware of God's presence giving your marriage the strength it needed—or of a time when having God as the third strand in your marriage might have made a huge difference.

- Think about your daily routine. When would be the best time to read the Bible together? When would be the best time(s) to pray? Also address the best place for the time you spend with your spouse and God.

- What Christian couple might serve as mentors for you for a while?

Chapter 16: The Most Important Thing of All

DISCUSS WITH YOUR SPOUSE

- Which of the following do you think will fall into place most naturally? And which of these steps do you expect to find most challenging? What can you do to minimize the challenge and maximize the chance of success?

  Do it daily.

  Keep it short.

  Keep things relaxed and comfortable.

  Consider reading a daily devotional book.

  Read from the Bible, especially scriptures relevant to your relationship with God and with each other.

  Pray together.

- At the heart of this book is this belief: "The daily seven minutes you spend getting closer to God and each other will be the most important—even the most crucial—seven minutes in your marriage." Share with your spouse your agreement and hopes . . . your skepticism and hesitancy . . . or the emotions you're feeling somewhere between those two extremes.

DISCUSS WITH YOUR GROUP

- What do you find helpful about the metaphor that marriage is like a growing garden? In what ways is spending regular time with God as essential to the nourishment of your spirit as regular meals are essential to the nourishment of your body?

- What can we do to keep from treating prayer and Bible reading as merely another item on a to-do list?

APPLICATION

- Find resources for Bible study and prayer time.

- What book of the Bible will you start to read together—or how will you determine what to read together?

- What approach to prayer would be most comfortable and meaningful to the two of you? The *7 Minute Marriage Solution Devotional Bible* could be exactly the resource you need.

If every day you approach these seven minutes as time you are investing in your mate and your God the blessings you receive in return will inspire you and enable you to become a selfless, serving, and loving spouse who makes marriage a joy.

May God bless you as you learn more and more each day how to cling to him and to each other.

TIPS FOR LEADERS

- Pray! Pray before every group meeting. Pray during every meeting. Pray after every meeting. May the Lord prepare hearts, soften hearts, transform hearts, and transform marriages.

- If you're comfortable doing so, open each meeting time with a brief prayer and close with a brief prayer. Consider delegating this responsibility.

- An icebreaker—especially the first week—will help people relax and start getting to know one another. Here are some suggestions: When/where did you first meet?; What made you ask for/go out on that second date?; Where is your favorite place to vacation—and why?; or What takes up most of your time during the week—and what do you like to do to relax?

- After you call the group together and get started, you may or may not choose to give spouses five minutes for "Follow Up on 7 Things to Do."

- Remind participants that what is shared in the group is shared with no one outside the group.

- Be respectful to the group members: start on time; end on time. In group discussions, do what you can to be sure people who want to respond have an opportunity, but let people know that participation is optional.

- Time will undoubtedly be an issue, so familiarize yourself with the questions and have an idea what to cut. Consider, for instance, leaving a "spouse" question for a couple to discuss or journal.

- God sovereignly brought this circle together. He knows the reasons why, but you don't. You may also not know how these husbands and wives are doing, what issues they're dealing with, how strong or precarious their relationship is. Give people the option to pass rather than answer.

- If participants have read the chapters, they may not come if the topic makes them too uncomfortable, if God's truth is too convicting. But if busy participants arrive without reading the material, some might possibly be surprised by the topic and find themselves entering shaky or volatile ground during the discussion times. Be prayerful. Be prepared: have, for instance, with a handout listing reliable marriage counselors and various easy-to-access resources (pastors, books, seminars, programs at local churches).

- Some of the "group" questions may also work as discussion topics for same-sex groups, but your meeting time may not allow for that additional dynamic. Perhaps, though, a certain lesson works well with a combination of "spouse" conversations plus "same-sex" rather than group conversations.

NOTES

Chapter 1: STOP CLINGING to Unrealistic Expectations

1. "Marriage in America: The Frayed Knot," *Economist*, May 24, 2007; http://www.economist.com/node/9218127.

2. Kathryn Jean Lopez, "Levi's Story: Retreating from Marriage in America," *National Review Online*, December 10, 2010; www.nationalreview.com/articles/254877/levi-s-story-interview.

Chapter 2: STOP OBSESSING on the Past

1. Milan and Kay Yerkovich, *How We Love* (Colorado Springs: Waterbrook Press, 2008).

Chapter 3: STOP DROWNING in Suspicion and Jealousy

1. John Townsend, "Building Trust," *Focus on the Family*, April 2008, http://www.focusonthefamily.com/marriage/divorce_and_infidelity/forgiveness_and_restoration/building_trust.aspx.

2. "Infidelity Statistics," InfidelityFacts, http://www.infidelityfacts.com/infidelity-statistics.html.

3. Ibid.

4. Ibid.

5. There are many Internet sources for this story. An interesting sidelight to this event was that a few years later, when Kaiser Wilhelm's actions led to World War I, someone quipped that Annie Oakley could have prevented the war by putting the bullet through the Kaiser's head instead of his cigarette. Responding to this quip, Annie reportedly wrote a letter to Kaiser Wilhelm requesting a second shot. She did not receive an answer.

6. John Townsend, "Building Trust."

7. Ibid.

Chapter 5: STOP SEETHING in Anger and Resentment

1. Richard P. Fitzgibbons, "The Angry Spouse," MaritalHealing.com, http://www.maritalhealing.com/conflicts/angryspouse.php.

2. These rules of engagement are adapted from the book, *A Lasting Promise: A Christian Guide to Fighting for Your Marriage* by Scott Stanley, Daniel Trathen, Savanna McCain, and Milt Bryan (San Francisco: Jossey-Bass, 1998).

Chapter 6: STOP TOLERATING Compulsions and Addictions

1. Stephen Arterburn and Fred Stoker with Mike Yorkey, *Every Man's Battle* (Colorado Springs: WaterBrook, 2009).

2. Cindy Wright, "The Christian Woman: Her Dirty Little Porn Secret," Marriage Missions International, http://www.marriagemissions.com/the-christian-woman-her-dirty-little-porn-secret/.

3. C. S. Lewis, *The Problem of Pain* (New York: Macmillan, 1962), 28–29.

Chapter 7: STOP FOCUSING Only on Your Interests

1. Elizabeth Dickson, "How to Turn Conflict into Intimacy," RelationshipRealizations.com, http://relationshiprealizations.com/psychotherapy-articles/how-to-turn-conflict-into-intimacy.htm.

2. Sarah Jane Glynn, "The New Breadwinners: 2010 Update: Rates of Women Supporting Their Families Economically Increased Since 2007," Center for American Progress, April 16, 2012, http://www.americanprogress.org/issues/labor/report/2012/04/16/11377/the-new-breadwinners-2010-update/.

Chapter 8: START EMBRACING Friendship and Fun

1. Alyson Weasley, "The Role of Friendship in Marriage," Focus on the Family, http://www.focusonthefamily.com/marriage/sex_and_intimacy/the_role_of_friendship_in_marriage.aspx.

2. Bill and Pam Farrel, *Red-Hot Monogamy* (Eugene, OR: Harvest House, 2006).

3. James R. White with Peter Kent, *The Best Sex of Your Life* (Fort Lee, NJ: Barricade Books, 1997) 91.

4. Bill and Pam Farrel, "Recreational Intimacy," Focus on the Family, http://www.focus onthefamily.com/marriage/daily_living/making-time-for-romance-and-intimacy/recreational-intimacy.aspx.

Chapter 9: START RESPONDING Romantically to Your Mate

1. Christopher West, *At the Heart of the Gospel* (New York: Image Books, 2012), 190.

2. Peter Paul Rubens, *Adam and Eve*, Peter Paul Rubens: The Complete Works, http://www.peterpaulrubens.org/Adam-and-Eve.html.

3. Lucas Cranach the Elder, *Eve*, Olga's Gallery, http://www.abcgallery.com/C/cranach/cranach66.html.

Chapter 11: START AFFIRMING Your Mate's Strengths

1. Adapted from Jim Bradford, "Marriage: Accepting, not Judging," Assemblies of God USA, February 1, 2012. http://agtv.ag.org/marriage_accepting_not_judging.

Chapter 12: START SPENDING Money Responsibly

1. Gary Smalley, *Making Love Last Forever* (Nashville: Thomas Nelson, 1997).

2. Dave Ramsey, "Money Talk: The 'You' in 'Unity' Is Silent," Focus on the Family, http://www.focusonthefamily.com/marriage/money_and_finances/pursuing_financial_unity/money_talk_the_you_in_unity_is_silent.aspx.

3. Crown Financial Ministries, "Financial Authority," Focus on the Family website, adapted from Larry Burkett, "Financial Authority in the Home," in *Biblical Principles Under Scrutiny* (Chicago: Moody, 1990), 177–179, http://www.focusonthefamily.com/marriage/money_and_finances/money_management_in_marriage/financial_authority.aspx.

4. Ben Woolsey and Matt Schulz, "Credit card statistics, industry facts, debt statistics," Credit Cards.com; http://www.creditcards.com/credit-card-news/credit-card-industry-facts-personal-debt-statistics-1276.php.

5. Carolyn MacInnes, "Big Dreams on a Small Budget," Focus on the Family, http://www.focusonthefamily.com/marriage/money_and_finances/money_management_in_marriage/big_dreams_on_a_small_budget.aspx.

Chapter 13: START PRACTICING Your Lifetime Vows

1. Emil Protalinski, "Facebook Blamed for 1 in 5 Divorces in the US," ZDNet, March 1, 2011, http://www.zdnet.com/blog/facebook/facebook-blamed-for-1-in-5-divorces-in-the-us/359.

2. Willard F. Harley, "The Four Rules for a Successful Marriage," Marriage Builders, accessed June 11, 2012, http://www.marriagebuilders.com/graphic/mbi3901_rules.html.

3. Adapted from Harley, "The Four Rules for a Successful Marriage."

4. "Major New Study: Does Divorce Make People Unhappy? Findings from a Study of Unhappy Marriages," undated press release, AmericanValues.org, http://www.americanvalues.org/html/r-unhappy_ii.html.

5. DivorceStatistics.org, accessed December 28, 2011.

6. Ed Cray, *General of the Army: George C. Marshall, Soldier and Statesman* (New York: W. W. Norton, 1990), 89.

Chapter 14: START SHOWING Respect No Matter What

1. C. S. Lewis, "The Weight of Glory" in *The Weight of Glory and Other Addresses* (New York: Macmillan, 1949), 19.

Chapter 15: The Three-Stranded Cord of Marriage

1. Harold G. Stigers, *A Commentary on Genesis* (Grand Rapids: Zondervan, 1976), 66.

About the Author

STEPHEN ARTERBURN is a best-selling and award-winning author with over eight million books in print. His popular titles include *Every Man's Battle* and *Healing Is a Choice*. He has also been the editor of ten Bible projects, including *The Life Recovery Bible*. Arterburn founded New Life Treatment Centers in 1988 and is currently host of the radio and television show *New Life Live*. In 1996 he started the successful traveling conference Women of Faith, which has been attended by more than four million people. He and his wife live with their five kids in Fishers, Indiana.

It's time for
New Life!
Hope in the storm, Help in the struggle

America's #1 Christian Counseling Call-in Show

New Life Live
WITH STEVE ARTERBURN

And his co-hosts:

Dr. Jill Hubbard

Dr. Dave Stoop

Dr. Henry Cloud

Dr. John Townsend

Dr. Sheri Denham

Rev. Milan Yerkovich

To be on the show, call 1-800-229-3000.

To find a station in your area, go to newlife.com or call 800-NEW-LIFE (639-5433)
also SiriusXM Satellite Radio on Channel 131 at 10:00AM PT

800-NEW-LIFE (639-5433)   **newlife.com**

NEW LIFE
MARRIAGE WEEKEND
WORKSHOP

 *Rejuvenate*   *Rescue*   *Restore*

There is hope for your marriage!

- Do you want the tools to make a great marriage?

- Do you need to repair love that's been broken?

- Do you want a deeper spiritual and emotional intimacy?

Designed to take the focus from what was and what might have been and onto the path of what is and what is to be. All workshop attendees will attend process groups where they will work on their issues of concern with a Christian counselor and fellow attendees.

for information or to register call

800-NEW-LIFE (639-5433) **newlife.com**

WORTHY
PUBLISHING

IF YOU ENJOYED THIS BOOK, WILL YOU CONSIDER
SHARING THE MESSAGE WITH OTHERS?

- Mention the book in a Facebook post, Twitter update, Pinterest pin, or blog post.

- Recommend this book to those in your small group, book club, workplace, and classes.

- Head over to facebook.com/NewLifeLive, "LIKE" the page, and post a comment as to what you enjoyed the most.

- Tweet "I recommend reading #7MinuteMarriageSolution by @SteveArterburn // @worthypub"

- Pick up a copy for someone you know who would be challenged and encouraged by this message.

- Write a review on amazon.com, bn.com, goodreads.com, or cbd.com.

You can subscribe to Worthy Publishing's
newsletter at worthypublishing.com.

WORTHY PUBLISHING
FACEBOOK PAGE

WORTHY PUBLISHING
WEBSITE